FLY AFRICA

FLY AFRICA

HOW AVIATION CAN GENERATE PROSPERITY ACROSS THE CONTINENT

ERIC KACOU
HASSAN EL-HOURY

LIONCREST
PUBLISHING

COPYRIGHT © 2017 ERIC KACOU & HASSAN EL-HOURY
All rights reserved.

FLY AFRICA
How Aviation Can Generate Prosperity Across the Continent

ISBN   978-1-61961-806-0 *Hardcover*
       978-1-61961-807-7 *Paperback*
       978-1-61961-808-4 *Ebook*

DEDICATION BY HASSAN

*I dedicate my first book to
my sons, Bassam, Kareem, and Ahmed;
their mother and their grandparents; and
their aunts, uncles, cousins, great-aunts, and great-uncles.
"You measure yourself by the people who measure themselves by you."*

DEDICATION BY ERIC

*I dedicate my second book to my daughter,
Maria, and my wife, Darline.*

CONTENTS

Introduction 11

Section One: The Aviation Situation in Africa
1. Poor Connections 31
2. Why Africa Must Fly to Rise 49

Section Two: Foundations of African Aviation
3. Stakeholders in Aviation 69
4. One Africa, Many Nations 87

Section Three: Opportunities in Aviation in Africa
5. Upgrading Aviation Infrastructure 109
6. Aviation Support Services in Africa 119
7. The Changing Face of Africa's Top Carriers 139

Section Four: Solutions for Aviation in Africa
8. Nurturing Aviation Champions in Africa 157
9. The Agenda for Aviation in Africa 179

Conclusion 195
Acknowledgments 199
About the Authors 201

AUTHORS' NOTE

Authoring a book brings many challenges, and coauthoring a book brings a few additional challenges. One of those is determining how best to express the voices of two separate people in print. Eventually, we settled on the following approach: Where we describe the individual experiences of Eric and Hassan, we've chosen to use the third person. Where we assert our shared viewpoint, we've chosen to use the first person. We hope these choices make our book as clear and readable as possible.

INTRODUCTION

In 2012, Hassan met an elderly woman in the business class lounge of Dubai International Airport. As travelers do, the two of them sparked up a conversation. The woman mentioned that her family had owned a boutique hotel in Mauritius for decades. Although moderately successful, the hotel was never lucrative.

When Emirates started flying an A380 to Mauritius in 2013, the hotel was transformed. Suddenly, Mauritius was on the map. It became an accessible destination from Europe, Africa, the Middle East, and even the United States. At the time she spoke to Hassan, this woman's hotel was fully booked year-round. She regularly hosted businesspeople, tourists, and family reunions. A single scheduled route completely altered her experience of running a hotel.

For Eric, the first time he realized the power of air connectivity to change lives was in August 1993, when he left Côte d'Ivoire to study business in Canada. That single flight opened horizons and possibilities he had never imagined. While similar educational opportunities were available in Côte d'Ivoire, he wouldn't have been exposed to the same range of experiences and professionals.

A large percentage of the world's business is conducted in English. For Eric, the ability to travel to North America and learn firsthand about the culture in which he was immersed changed the way he understood the world and influenced the way he conducted business. It introduced him to new models and ideas that have informed his perspective. He credits the experience with making him far more effective in his chosen sphere, and with introducing him to people he would never have encountered in Africa.

Since then, Eric has traveled to more than seventy countries for work, his studies, and as a tourist. In his role as the cofounder and CEO of Entrepreneurial Solutions Partners (ESPartners), he has advised the leaders of more than a dozen African and Caribbean nations, corporations, and development institutions. Without aviation, it would be impossible for him to fulfill his professional potential. It's also unlikely he would ever have met Hassan, and the book you're currently reading might never have come into existence.

Hassan, meanwhile, has channeled his love of aviation into his work with National Aviation Services (NAS). As the group CEO, he has spearheaded NAS's expansion into more than thirty locations, including international airports in India, Afghanistan, Tanzania, Rwanda, Côte d'Ivoire, Liberia, Egypt, Uganda, and Morocco. Under his leadership, NAS has received the prestigious Best Ground Handling Company in Emerging Markets award on multiple occasions.

Aviation impacts all our lives, on both the macro- and the microlevel. The smartphones we've come to rely on so heavily crisscross the planet on airplanes. Much of the food we eat is transported by air. A lot of products that are integral parts of our lives come to us through air travel, from electronics to medicines.

The ability to travel freely has dramatically changed our understanding of life. Twenty years ago, it was common to plan travel months ahead. It felt like a big deal. Today, your authors travel seven or eight times per month. That kind of schedule simply wouldn't be possible by land or sea. Only aviation allows for such a high level of mobility.

Both your authors recognize how fortunate they are. Aviation has changed our lives, yet this possibility is still denied to hundreds of millions of Africans. The reason we are writing this book is because we believe that unleashing the potential of aviation in Africa will transform the lives of ordinary people.

There are surely hundreds of stories of businesses that have already been transformed due to enhanced connectivity. We believe that a vibrant aviation sector is essential for African economies, as a whole, to reach their fullest potential.

AN OVERVIEW OF AFRICAN AVIATION

Africa is a single continent, but it consists of fifty-four separate countries. Across the continent, there is a huge disparity between countries that operate a relatively developed aviation industry and others where services are far more limited. In a few cases, there are countries with no aviation industry whatsoever.

On the other end of the spectrum are countries such as Ethiopia, South Africa, Kenya, and Egypt, which function as regional hubs. Ethiopia, for example, has a strong national carrier that accounts for more than 70 percent of flights into the country. Ghana, on the other hand, has taken a different approach, developing a vibrant aviation sector without a national carrier. Passenger volumes and cargo are mostly shared between international carriers, with a few small, locally owned airlines claiming a small percentage.

When we investigated the situation more closely, we realized we could categorize the aviation industry in different countries in terms of how well-developed the aviation sector is, both in terms of economic impact (e.g., jobs, receipts, contribution to

GDP) and in terms of connectivity to other nations. We wanted to understand the divergent levels of service and use our findings to present a picture of the aviation industry across the continent, one that can be used by decision makers to improve aviation within their own countries. To do this, we make liberal use of statistics, especially in the early chapters of this book. Please bear with us as we paint a picture of African aviation.

Africa is a colossal place with a massive aviation sector. Geographically, Africa's landmass is larger than Europe, the United States, and India combined, and is home to approximately one and a half billion people. At the time of writing, it contains 731 airports and 419 airlines. This is an enormous number. Yet, there are very few large, successful airlines across the continent. Only about ten companies carry more than one million passengers per year, and only about twelve offer intercontinental flights. It's an unfortunate fact that although Africans make up more than 12 percent of the world's population, they are fewer than 3 percent of the world's passengers. African aviation is an industry operating far below its potential.

The continent is also amazingly diverse, in every sense of the word. Each of the continent's fifty-four countries has its own history, its own culture, and its own future. There's a tendency to discuss Africa as though it's a single country, like China, Turkey, or Brazil. Yet, each country needs to be addressed individually. Nonetheless, there are four major themes characterizing African aviation.

The first is poor connectivity. Passengers wishing to fly from one midsized city to another almost always need to travel via a third or even a fourth city. Some travelers originating in Africa even fly through Europe or the Middle East to connect to another city through Africa. Hassan, for example, recently wanted to travel from Abidjan to Kampala, both economic powerhouses. With no direct flights between them, however, the quickest route, and the one Hassan chose, was to fly to Istanbul and reconnect. Scenarios like this double or triple journey times on many routes.

The second theme is high ticket prices. It's expensive traveling to and from Africa. It's also expensive to travel within Africa. The third is that aviation in Africa is dominated by foreign carriers. The likes of Air France, KLM, British Airways, Emirates, Lufthansa, and Turkish Airlines pepper African skies, and most African carriers are currently unable to compete with them. It's true there are a few African airlines with the volume and breadth of the carriers mentioned above, but only a few. These include Kenya Airways, South African Airways, Ethiopian, EgyptAir, and increasingly Royal Air Maroc. With these few exceptions, other carriers are much smaller, and they are overshadowed by the larger international carriers.

Finally, the fourth primary characteristic of aviation in Africa is the disparity in quality. Dar es Salaam in Tanzania is a major metropolitan city, but you might not believe that if you visited the airport. It's old, running over capacity, and the infrastructure is poorly maintained; however, as of 2017, the country is completing a new terminal that should remedy this situation. On the other hand, the airport at Abidjan in Côte d'Ivoire is brand new, well maintained, and exceptionally well organized and well managed. The disparity is huge. The same goes for the disparity between African aviation and the rest of the world.

Nonetheless, aviation in Africa has evolved significantly. According to statistics from the World Bank, the number of passengers in Africa has skyrocketed from about five million in 1970 to more than one hundred million in 2015. Thirty or forty years ago, most of the traffic from the continent to other areas of the planet was to Europe or the United States. Now, there's a lot of traffic between Africa and the Middle East and between Africa and Asia, as well as between Africa and the rest of the world. Thus, hubs that serve all these destinations have grown considerably and done well. Relationships between African cities and countries and their Asian and Middle Eastern counterparts have strengthened and deepened. As intra-African trade has increased and visa restrictions have decreased, travel *within* the continent has also grown significantly.

One example of this phenomenon is Nairobi. As China and Dubai emerged as global trade centers, African businesspeople began traveling regularly to these places to acquire merchandise. Many Africans travel to India for medical treatment or to study. A lot of these flights pass through Nairobi.

In total, 36 percent of Africa's international traffic passes through just three hubs: Johannesburg, Nairobi, and Addis Ababa. Of South African Airways' total traffic, 33 percent is international, while 70 percent of Kenya Airways' traffic and an enormous 83 percent of Ethiopian Airways' traffic is international.

Another disparity in Africa lies between the east and the west of the continent. In both eastern and southern Africa, there is a history of aviation. In countries such as Ethiopia and Kenya, the history of the airline industry is long and distinguished. They have been centers for extremely well-run airlines for decades. In Ethiopia, Emperor Haile Selassie decided to invest in the country's national carrier more than seventy years ago. The country has remained committed to its airline ever since, despite wars and political challenges.

In West Africa and Central Africa, however, many countries have made unsuccessful attempts to establish national and regional airlines. Many of them failed due to poor management, while others were affected by the dominance of existing European airlines. They feel much closer to Europe and much more accessible from a European base than their counterparts in the east and the south. In addition, many of the economies in southern Africa and eastern Africa are more vibrant than those in West Africa and Central Africa.

Broadly speaking, East African national carriers are more successful than those in West Africa. The former is home to Ethiopian, Kenyan, and EgyptAir, while RwandAir is emerging as another East African airline to be reckoned with. The latter has Arik Air, Air Côte d'Ivoire, ASKY of Togo, and Royal Air Maroc. All four of these West African carriers combined carry fewer passengers than Ethiopian alone.

These factors have made it difficult for national and regional airlines to emerge. Many of those that *have* succeeded have done so by partnering with Air France-KLM. Today, Nigeria is the foremost economic power on the continent. Yet, it has never become a strong hub or launched a national airline. Nigeria's decision to turn over the management of Arik Air to Ethiopian in August 2017 further exemplifies this situation.

Numerous African cities aspire to become hubs. Yet, they are competing with existing hubs through which an enormous percentage of flights are already routed. We regularly meet friends and colleagues by chance in Nairobi, Johannesburg, and Addis Ababa, simply because those airports are essential stops for travelers wanting to reach many different destinations.

Due to these challenges, the African aviation sector is far

from reaching its potential. Between 2001 and 2007, at least thirty-one African airlines ceased operations. In total, dozens of airlines have launched on the continent and subsequently ceased to exist, many of them in Nigeria.[1] No sooner has one come into being than, it seems, another has failed. This presents a major problem for the industry. Without continuity, it's challenging to build a strong aviation sector. Globally recognized airlines, such as British Airways and Air France, took decades to build. Many African airlines last less than a year.

The reasons for these failures are somewhat consistent. Many have suffered from a poor safety record. For some, this has manifested in a major disaster, which forced them to shut down. For others, it resulted in their being barred from European airspace, limiting their potential markets. Disagreements between partners have often escalated into fights, causing them to shut down the business. Some airlines are founded for political reasons and supported by powerful patrons. Politics is notoriously unstable, so when the conditions shift, many airlines cannot adapt to the new realities. In addition to all these problems, African airlines regularly face currency problems, mismanagement issues, and governance struggles.

This last represents an especially profound challenge. Aviation is a difficult sector—airlines fail regularly in the developed world—but it's *especially* difficult in Africa. Governments have

---

[1] "List of defunct airlines of Africa," Wikipedia, accessed October 13, 2017, https://en.wikipedia.org/wiki/List_of_defunct_airlines_of_Africa

comparatively little experience understanding and managing the sector, making an already-complex sector an even harder environment in which to succeed.

LEADING COUNTRIES IN AFRICA BY PASSENGERS CARRIED BOTH DOMESTIC AND INTERNATIONAL IN 2016 (MILLIONS)

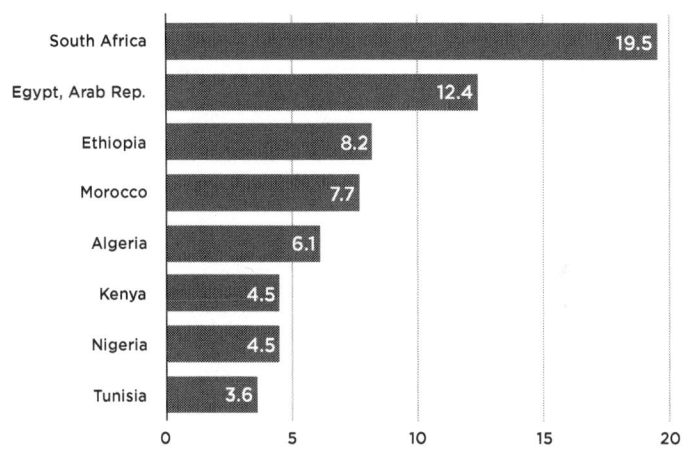

South Africa	19.5
Egypt, Arab Rep.	12.4
Ethiopia	8.2
Morocco	7.7
Algeria	6.1
Kenya	4.5
Nigeria	4.5
Tunisia	3.6

Source: International Civil Aviation Organization, Civil Aviation Statistics of the World and ICAO staff estimates.

LEADING AIRLINES IN AFRICA BY FLEET AS OF DECEMBER 2016 (IN UNITS)

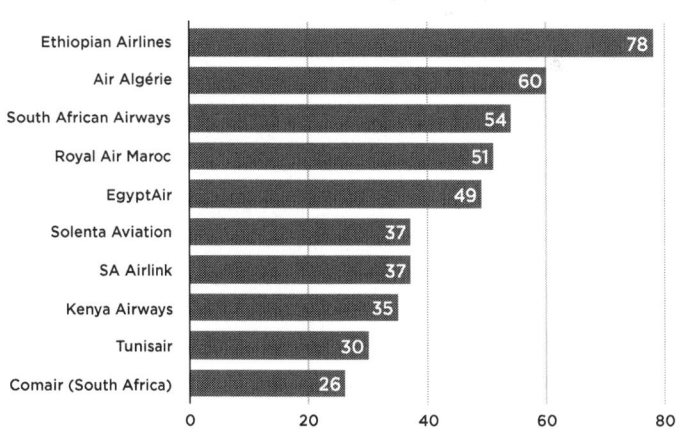

Ethiopian Airlines	78
Air Algérie	60
South African Airways	54
Royal Air Maroc	51
EgyptAir	49
Solenta Aviation	37
SA Airlink	37
Kenya Airways	35
Tunisair	30
Comair (South Africa)	26

Source: Statista, 2017, consulter le 24/09/2017; https://www.statista.com/statistics/687967/airlines-in-africa-fleet-size/

THE MASSIVE POTENTIAL OF AFRICAN AVIATION

Historically, aviation in Africa has primarily been viewed as a privilege of the rich. Airlines have been a way for wealthy people to take lavish vacations, while governments have tended to seize upon the potential to generate tax revenue. To an extent, this situation persists. Departure taxes in the region of US$100 aren't uncommon. To the rich, these taxes appear minimal, while governments are motivated to maximize their revenue.

The following tables compare the costs of flying within Africa and flying within Europe, using six sample routes. Prices are based on the cheapest available flights, departing on January 15, 2018, and returning on March 15, 2018.

ROUTE	DISTANCE (KM)	FARE (ECONOMY, USD)	FARE (BUSINESS, USD)	TAXES AND CHARGES
Addis Ababa to Nairobi	1,166.74	73	871	166
Addis Ababa to Abidjan	4,732.95	708	2,161	206
Nairobi to Khartoum	1,940.82	356	1,024	259
Nairobi to Kigali	753.15	176	625	136
Abidjan to Lagos	817.52	386	927	166
Lusaka to Luanda	1,805.63	422	1,300	163

ROUTE	DISTANCE (KM)	FARE (ECONOMY, USD)	FARE (BUSINESS, USD)	TAXES AND CHARGES
London to Paris	344.39	33	150	120
London to Istanbul	2,505.68	7	239	106
Paris to Rome	1,103.98	47	868	86
Paris to Lisbon	1,475.73	20	688	66
Frankfurt to Amsterdam	366.92	40	213	203
Istanbul to Stockholm	2,203.13	146	804	37

As you can see, intracontinental flights within Africa are far more expensive than comparable routes in Europe. Our research revealed that, across more than a dozen routes, one dollar spent in economy class in Africa enables passengers to travel 6.04 km. The same dollar spent in Europe propels passengers an average of 44.44 km. In business class, a dollar buys 1.49 km of travel in Africa and 3.98 km in Europe.

The difference in taxes is not so pronounced. In fact, European business class taxes average $13.74 per 100 km, while African business class taxes average $12.46 per 100 km. For European economy class travel, taxes average $8.95 per 100 km. In Africa, the number is $12.38 per 100 km.

For middle-class travelers, however, these taxes are both punitive and shortsighted. Aviation is an important economic tool with a broad impact. The sector supports tourists, business travelers, patients, doctors, investors, family members who live a long way from one another, professors, researchers, and many other professionals.

Almost every sector of society is supported by strong aviation infrastructure and hampered by poor aviation infrastructure. Finance ministers looking to bolster revenues in the sector may see little alternative to imposing high departure taxes in an effort to keep aviation alive. Yet, this approach may be counterproductive, driving down passenger numbers and depressing the broader economy. Transport infrastructure alone doesn't trigger economic growth, but it's a necessary precondition. It plays a key role in complementing policies that lift living standards. The proliferation of air services improves access to social services and increases personal mobility.

In addition, aviation can be a source of jobs, one of the key challenges for many African countries. This is true in the industry itself. Aviation requires skilled and semiskilled labor. Every person who comes in contact with an aircraft must be trained in certain basic functions, such as airport security, whether they work in the aircraft or at the airport. More broadly, working in aviation can be a route out of poverty and toward jobs requiring more qualifications.

The sector is also highly labor-intensive. To use banking as a counterpoint, one person can move billions of dollars at the click of a button. In aviation, every aircraft requires pilots, cabin crew, cleaners, porters, check-in agents, refueling technicians, mechanics, and engineers. In 2017, the aviation sector in Africa directly supports approximately seven million jobs. Indirectly, the number is much higher.[2] In summary, aviation supports an entire ecosystem of people.

The indirect influence of aviation also contributes to its economic impact. Jobs in the tourism sector, for example, depend upon airlines bringing people to the places where those jobs exist. Many jobs in tourism are *also* labor-intensive, meaning that there's more work to be done, requiring more people. Overall, then, aviation supports a large number of jobs, both within the industry and externally, and can play a key role in meeting Africa's employment challenges.

Every single country in Africa is looking for a way to develop its aviation sector. When leaders talk about emergence, however, what they often mean is they want their countries to become middle-income nations. Some of them grew up poor, fought for independence, and suffered torture and imprisonment. Seeing their countries attain a moderate level of prosperity means a great deal to them. Those who already lead middle-income nations aspire to see their countries grow even faster.

---

[2] Raphael Kuuchi, "Africa's Potential Is Sky High—and the Airline Industry Is Key," World Economic Forum, May 11, 2016, https://www.weforum.org/agenda/2016/05/africa-s-potential-is-sky-high-and-the-airline-industry-is-key/

Sometimes, this impulse finds its fulfillment in projects with a doubtful economic rationale. Consider the King Mswati III International Airport, originally known as the Sikuphe International Airport, in Swaziland. Built at a cost of between US$300 and US$600 million, with the intention of meeting the country's Millennium Development Goals, the airport needs to serve an estimated 360,000 passengers annually for the project to break even.

Unfortunately, the concrete impact of the airport on the life of the average Swazi is yet to emerge. The airport has not yet contributed to a rise in passenger numbers. In a country of 1.2 million people, 60 percent of whom earn less than a dollar per day, the number of prospective passengers is limited. At the time of writing, the only airline serving the airport is South Africa's Airlink, although Swaziland has announced plans to launch its own airline, serving ten destinations in Africa and Asia, shortly.

Aviation is so much more than a *symbol* of prosperity. It can be part of the solution, the route toward that prosperity. If African aviation is going to reach its potential, it will be essential for both business and government leaders both to undergo a shift in mindset and to gain a deeper understanding of how to succeed in aviation. Until they see aviation as a tool to create growth, it will be difficult for African nations to both develop a potent aviation sector and harness the economic benefits of the industry.

There are signs that some African countries are beginning to understand this. The African Union Commission (AUC) Agenda 2063 acknowledges the importance of aviation. The Republic of South Sudan, Africa's newest country, has made upgrading its airport an integral part of its economic development strategy. Soon after achieving independence, it secured funding to build a brand-new passenger terminal at Juba International Airport and repair the airport's ailing runway. The deputy transport minister, Mayom Kuoc Malek, referred to the construction of the new passenger terminal as "our highest priority." As of 2017, South Sudan is plagued by a tragic civil war, and most government institutions are suspended. Nonetheless, the airport continues to function because it's needed by all factions, including international aid agencies, foreign dignitaries and ambassadors, as well as ordinary citizens. Rwanda, too, has broken ground on new construction—namely, the state-of-the-art $800 million Bugesera Airport, which promises to be a major asset in its economic transformation strategy.

As you read this book, we hope you'll see both a diagnosis of the issues facing African aviation and concrete proposals for solutions. We'll use a mixture of data and stories to make our points about the value of the sector and to outline the enormous opportunities that exist in aviation on the continent. The challenges facing African aviation are real, but if we can bridge that gap, the opportunities are enormous, both for Africa and for the rest of the world.

The repercussions of a healthy aviation sector in Africa would be felt everywhere. It would mean more African tourists in Europe, more African businesspeople in the Middle East, and more African students in the United States. That, in turn, would portend a new relationship between Africa and the rest of the world. In this book, we aim to offer both a realistic appraisal of the current situation and an optimistic vision of what's possible when we unleash the potential of aviation in Africa.

SECTION ONE

THE AVIATION SITUATION IN AFRICA

CHAPTER ONE

POOR CONNECTIONS

As you're probably aware, the World Economic Forum runs a major event in Davos, Switzerland every year. Less well known is the fact that the organization also hosts regional events in Europe, Africa, and other locations. In 2016, Rwanda won the right to host the event. President Paul Kagame himself led the charge. It was a big moment for the country—an opportunity to show the world how much it had developed since the terrible genocide of 1994.

Within the country, the organization was perfect. From hotels and the conference center to transportation and security, everything worked without a hitch. The only problem was flying *to* Rwanda. From Dubai, for example, a major regional hub, there was only one daily flight to Kigali. Naturally, with so many people visiting the capital, this flight booked up long before the conference.

This left unsuspecting attendees with a number of unappealing choices. They could arrive several days early, when flights were still available. They could miss the first day of the conference and catch the following day's flight. Alternatively, they were faced with the option of taking a tortuous route incorporating overnight travel, making one or more stops, or even missing the conference altogether. Just as Rwanda was flexing its economic muscles, the need for improved aviation links to and from the country came into sharp focus.

COMPARING AFRICA WITH OTHER REGIONS

This chapter will explore the many ways in which African aviation falls short of its counterparts on other continents, and the consequences of those shortfalls. Unfortunately, investigating the data makes it impossible to avoid the conclusion that Africa lags far behind most other regions in the quality, safety, and cost of aviation services. The continent suffers from a lack of paved runways, a dearth of competition, low efficiency, poor regulation, and limited private sector involvement.

In the 1960s, as many African countries celebrated their independence, several chose to start their own state-owned airlines. Fifty years later, the world has evolved to favor privately owned airlines. Africa, however, has not caught up with this trend. Most of the continent's airlines, including all the major carriers, are state owned in some way.

This approach probably plays a part in the relatively low profitability of the African aviation industry. The International Air Transport Association (IATA) estimates that, in 2017, the airline industry worldwide will generate profits close to US$30 billion. The Asia-Pacific region, the most profitable, will register a profit of more than $6.3 billion, with Europe reaching approximately $5.6 billion. Africa, by contrast, is expected to post a net loss of $800 million. A symptom of this problem is the low penetration of low-cost carriers (LCCs) in Africa. Throughout Europe and North America, LCCs serve a significant proportion of the market, while in Africa, they remain rare.

In 2014, IATA reported that LCCs carried a total of 1.16 billion passengers, representing 26 percent of the global market. In 2013, however, African LCCs represented only 9 percent of the total annual seats sold across the continent.[3] As yet, then, few successful African LCCs exist, although the number is increasing. In 2015, four LCCs were launched in Africa: Fastjet Zimbabwe, yafrica.com Namibia, FlyEgypt, and Skywise. In 2014, they saw three launches: yafrica.com Zimbabwe, FlySafair, and Jambojet.

---

[3] *Africa Wings Magazine*, Issue 32, March 31, 2016, https://issuu.com/afraa/docs/africa_wings_32_/4

Air travel in Africa is exceptionally expensive. Traveling from Paris to Mumbai, for example, can cost as little as US$93. A similar ticket from Paris to Luanda in Angola retails at approximately $2,000. Paris to Dubai costs about $200, while a ticket from Paris to Addis Ababa is roughly $600. A similar dynamic is visible when comparing intracontinental flights. The cheapest ticket we found between London and Paris was a mere $12. Between Addis Ababa and Dar es Salaam, a similar distance, the cheapest flight was $400.

As the example of the World Economic Forum discussed above illustrates, connectivity in Africa is a persistent issue. Between Lusaka in Zambia and Abidjan in Côte d'Ivoire, for example, there are no direct flights. Passengers must transit between a second country, or even a third. In Europe, this is never a concern. There are direct flights between all capital cities.

These limitations create a vicious circle. The poor state of African aviation makes air travel on the continent economically unattractive. This, in turn, makes it hard to find the money for improvements, so the sector remains stagnant. Without investment to finance better service, it's hard for African airlines to attract more passengers. Without passengers, it's hard for the airlines to finance investment.

As discussed in the introduction, a successful aviation sector has a positive impact on many other aspects of the economy.

Naturally, the reverse is also true. Africa's underdeveloped aviation infrastructure hinders the ability of other sectors to operate effectively.

Given the size of the continent and the number of inhabitants, the African aviation sector is too small and underdeveloped. Its small size prevents it from generating as many jobs as it could, while its underdevelopment exacerbates the problem. Stakeholders and infrastructure are not as successful as they could be in wringing the most out of the sector. It should be remembered, however, that this doesn't represent a decline. There was no golden age of African aviation. This is encouraging, because it leads us to believe that—with intelligence and foresight—the continent can rise and fulfill its potential.

Worldwide seat capacity increased by 6.3 percent in 2015, with every major world region experiencing growth of 4.6 percent or above. All regions exceeded their respective GDP forecasts. The Africa/Middle East region, with GDP per capita running at 62.4 percent below the world average, represented only 11.8 percent of the world's available seat miles (ASM) during 2015. Nonetheless, the region recorded the highest ASM growth—10.3 percent—of the five major regions during the same period.[4]

---

[4] Reyyan Demir, "Airline Economic Analysis 2015-2016, by Oliver Wyman," Slideshare, February 10, 2016, https://www.slideshare.net/reyyandemir/oliver-wyman-airline-economic-analysis-2015-2016

When assessing the health of the African aviation sector, however, this number may be misleading. Of the total capacity of the Africa/Middle East region, the Middle East represents more than 72 percent. It's true that GDP growth rates are higher in Africa than in the Middle East. In 2017, average GDP growth in Africa is estimated to reach 5.9 percent, two percentage points higher than the Middle East.

While these statistics seem impressive, GDP levels are much higher in the Middle East than in Africa. Africa starts from a much lower base. This is illustrated by the fact that ASM growth is lower in Africa than the Middle East—3.9 percent as opposed to 10.3 percent in the region overall.

The total number of departures grew by 4.9 percent, but the number of seats per departure decreased, suggesting that smaller airplanes are becoming more prevalent. This may indicate that smaller, younger carriers are entering the sector and experiencing some success. Long-established carriers such as British Airways tend to use large aircraft, while smaller carriers lease smaller planes to fly short-haul routes.

According to a report from the World Economic Forum, Africa spends 3.5 percent of GDP on infrastructure. This may seem like a lot, but it pales in comparison with the 8.6 percent spent by China during its high-growth years between 1992 and 2013.

High transport and insurance costs also combine to stifle African growth. Exporting goods from Africa adds, on average, 30 percent to the price, according to the United Nations (UN) Economic Commission for Africa. For landlocked countries, such as Rwanda, Malawi, and Chad, this figure can reach 50 percent and compares unfavorably with the average for other developing countries at only 9 percent.

The low per capita GDP levels in Africa suggest that even the amount of growth already recorded is not yet enough to free up space in personal budgets for airline travel. Increasing personal wealth in the region further, however, could unlock tremendous growth potential. As disposable income increases, one of the sectors in which people naturally choose to spend money is airline services.

VISA CHALLENGES FOR AFRICANS

When Hassan was at the World Economic Forum in Rwanda, he met a young Rwandan woman with big ambitions. At one stage, she mentioned to Hassan she wanted to visit Angola, but she faced a frustrating ordeal. With no Angolan embassy in Rwanda, she would have needed to travel to a neighboring country just to *apply* for an Angolan visa. In addition, there was no option for her to apply online or by mail.

In practice, this meant that she would have needed to take at least two or three days of her life to secure a visa for Angola. First, in Rwanda, she would have needed to apply for a visa to a neighboring country. Only once she reached that country would she have been able to apply for a visa to Angola. In a worst-case scenario, she might have found herself waiting in another country, which she didn't even want to visit, for as long as a week or more.

Europeans and North Americans can travel within Africa more easily than Africans themselves. Canadians and citizens of the United States need visas to travel to 45 percent of African countries. They can procure visas on arrival in 35 percent of African countries and travel visa-free to 20 percent of African countries.

Most Africans require visas to enter 55 percent of other African countries, with visas on arrival available for 25 percent and visa-free access possible in another 20 percent. Some African passports offer even less mobility. Citizens of Nigeria and Cameroon, for example, are especially restricted. The most challenging countries to enter are those in North Africa and Central Africa, with the Democratic Republic of the Congo (DRC) exceptionally difficult to enter.

In West Africa, the Economic Community of West African States (ECOWAS) was formed to remove some of the barriers to travel. Member states have signed a protocol facilitating travel between themselves. In some ways, this is a risky move. Refugees may be encouraged to leave their own countries in search of a better life elsewhere. Côte d'Ivoire, for example, receives a lot of economic migrants from Burkina Faso. Nonetheless, the overall impact of making it easier to travel is positive.

Visa issues are shared throughout African nations. Fortunately, many African leaders, including President Kagame of Rwanda, are actively promoting a visa-free Africa for Africans and lending support to the AU Passport, which will probably debut in 2018. Initially, it will be available to diplomats and frequent travelers, with the potential to expand it if the scheme proves popular and successful.

Visas are a thorny issue. While they are undoubtedly cumbersome, there are good reasons why countries require visitors to acquire them. Visa policy may be shaped by security concerns, political considerations, or economic policy. Nonetheless, there's no reason to make it painful and difficult for ordinary citizens to obtain visas. In the twenty-first century, it should be possible for all countries to operate online visa application systems.

Another problem is that frequent travelers are often restricted to single-entry visas, instead of multiple-entry visas. For people who do business in a country other than their own, this makes their lives unnecessarily difficult. They are forced to go in person to embassies and consulates, receive visas with limited validity, and undergo the entire process again the next time they wish to visit. For business travelers, it makes far more sense to offer multiple-entry visas with a validity of a year or longer. Ultimately, it would be preferable to eliminate all barriers to travel. As an intermediate step, however, African countries that wish to encourage commerce and tourism must make it easier for people to apply for visas.

According to passportindex.com, the strongest African passport to hold comes from the Seychelles, ranking twenty-ninth in the world. Holders of Seychelles passports can access 137 countries visa-free. The next strongest is the Mauritian passport, ranking thirty-third and giving holders visa-free access to 131 countries. Your authors hold Lebanese (Hassan) and Ivorian (Eric) passports, ranked eighty-eighth and seventy-fourth, respectively. Even citizens of North Korea travel more freely than holders of Lebanese passports. Until it becomes easier for Africans to travel within Africa, it's difficult to see how the aviation sector can make significant progress.

INTERCONNECTED CHALLENGES EXACERBATE THE PROBLEMS

The multiple challenges faced by the African aviation sector cohere into a vicious circle, with each part of the industry having an impact on related areas. The lack of demand for aviation services, for example, means that African aviation companies lack revenue and purchasing power. This makes it harder for them to upgrade infrastructure and airplanes, contributing to a poor safety record. Naturally, people don't want to fly with airlines that have a poor safety record, further depressing demand. In this section, we'll discuss each of these challenges individually, then connect them together to illustrate a way forward.

As discussed previously, connectivity within Africa is limited. A passenger wishing to travel from Uganda to Côte d'Ivoire will find themselves passing through Ethiopia, Kenya, or perhaps Rwanda. They may wait twelve hours for a connecting flight.

Moreover, the safety record of many African airlines is at best questionable and at worst alarming, which discourages people from traveling. The International Civil Aviation Organization (ICAO) accident statistics from 2016 rank Africa as the most dangerous region in which to travel by air, with 7.3 accidents per million departures. This compares with 3 accidents per million departures in Europe and a global rate of 2.8 accidents per million departures.

Someone living in one of Nigeria's or the DRC's more remote cities and wanting to reach Lagos or Abuja will find themselves traveling in an aircraft that is many decades old, on an airline with a poor safety record. They will probably be uncomfortable and, assuming they reach their destination safely, the lack of entertainment system and disappointing food will likely leave them dissatisfied. We've spoken to passengers from both Nigeria and the DRC who've told us stories about smoke emanating from parts of the cabin and malfunctioning engines making abnormal sounds.

Airlines flying such routes are often faced with another obstacle: unfair competition and lax regulatory regimes. They may be underwritten by governments who are themselves not creditworthy. This places the airlines in the difficult position of not being able to upgrade their aircraft and, as mentioned above, struggling to attract more passengers.

Just as African airlines have trouble enticing more passengers, they're also rarely the first choice for trained pilots and staff. The airline business is growing globally, so good African pilots are looking to Europe and the Middle East for employment. This leads to a huge shortage of pilots in Africa, with the best from the diaspora taking jobs abroad.

Another problem for the sector is fuel cost. Almost a quarter of African countries are landlocked, which makes transporting fuel difficult and expensive. Bringing fuel to Uganda, South Sudan, and Burkina Faso, for example, requires land journeys across dangerous terrain. Naturally, this drives up fuel costs.

The age of many African aircraft has another drawback here. Their fuel consumption is higher than modern aircraft, making them more expensive to run. They pass this cost on to their passengers, increasing the price of tickets.

According to the *Journal of Transport Geography*, the cost of landing a two hundred-ton aircraft in Nairobi or Johannesburg is three to five times more than landing the same aircraft in London. In London, the fee paid to airport authorities is US$500. In Nairobi, it's $1,500, while in Johannesburg, $2,500. Inevitably, this also contributes to high ticket prices.[5]

The issues described in this section feed off one another and bring down the entire sector. In an industry as complex and sophisticated as aviation, it's essential that a number of pieces be in place. Visa policies must encourage people to travel. Airline safety records must allow people to feel comfortable setting foot on planes. Routes must be coordinated to allow people to reach their destinations in reasonable time. When one of these pieces isn't in place, it affects the desirability of air travel as a whole. This chokes off revenue streams and leads to further deficiencies.

While many governments would like to improve the situation, the detailed analysis that precedes construction projects in more developed aviation sectors is often hard to find. In Europe

---

5   Stephan Heinz and John F. O'Connell, "Air Transport in Africa: Toward Sustainable Business Models for African Airlines, *Journal of Transport Geography*, 31 (October 2016): 72-83, https://dspace.lib.cranfield.ac.uk/bitstream/1826/9701/3/Air_transport_in_Africa_toward_sustainable_business_models_for_African_airlines-2013.pdf

or America, construction of a new airport would be examined from every angle, with rigorous demand and feasibility studies. In Africa, the lack of this analysis often leads to suboptimal decision making. This problem is exacerbated when governments seek advice from stakeholders, constructors, and other interest groups who may have a vested interest in undertaking large, expensive projects.

Many African governments invest hundreds of millions of dollars in airports, hoping to recoup the cost through taxing travelers. They have witnessed the success of Dubai as an aviation hub, and they want to emulate that success. They may not realize, however, how many factors have contributed to Dubai's success. It has taken excellent infrastructure, an appropriate economic model, and strong leadership.

For example, Dubai started by offering airlines subsidized fuel, attracting them to route their planes through the airport. Dubai has built a reputation through commitment and investment, a path that many small African countries are ill-placed to emulate. Every country has its own history and its own future, and it follows that each country requires a unique vision of how it wishes to develop over the coming decades.

African aviation also suffers from a lack of credit card penetration across the continent. In Europe or the United States, travelers routinely book tickets online. In Africa, this isn't the case. Many passengers must purchase tickets through travel agents, who take an average commission of 7 percent. This system also renders the airlines dependent on travel agents to distribute tickets.

For the travel agents, however, this arrangement is not positive. Their networks of customers are often people they've known for many years, maybe even family members. To secure tickets, these people may rely on favors, promising to repay the cost of fares at a later date. This can work out well, but it can leave travel agents waiting for weeks, even months, to be repaid.

One of the reasons why passenger charges in African airports tend to be so high is that many lack the ecosystems familiar in most airports around the world. Imagine a major airport and you'll probably envisage a parking facility, an airport mall, places to eat and drink, car rental agencies, tour operators, and bureaus de change.

Each of these outlets pays royalties to airport authorities, reducing the need to impose high passenger charges. A lot of African countries don't seem to understand how effective this approach can be to raise revenue. In Uganda, for example, it's forbidden for nonpassengers to enter the airport. This makes it impossible for friends and family to accompany travelers to the airport and spend money while they're there.

Finally, a lot of African governments perceive running a national carrier as an issue of national sovereignty. Mozambique, for example, protects its national carrier at the expense of its passengers and the country's citizens. The airline is subsidized, which discourages competition and leads to higher airfares. This has the broader impact of hindering the development of tourism in the country.

Some African countries, however, have opened their skies. Both Ghana and Uganda, for example, have eschewed national carriers in favor of creating free, competitive environments. They've taken the role of regulator and refrained from running airlines. At the time of writing, however, Uganda is considering restarting a national carrier.

Protectionism inflates ticket prices further. In 2006, for example, traveling between Johannesburg in South Africa and Maputo in Mozambique was 163 percent more expensive than traveling the equivalent distance within South Africa.

SIGNS OF POSITIVE CHANGE

Despite these many challenges, there are signs of positive change. Uganda's minister of tourism abandoned a proposal to introduce a mandatory US$25 emergency medical insurance charge for inbound air travelers. In Senegal, the fiscal stamp tax was reduced from $11.80 to $3.37 in 2015. These moves show that, in the long term, some countries understand that levying high taxes on aviation passengers is counterproductive.

The problem is systemic. Investing in aviation is a marathon, not a sprint. Yet, governments are elected for a few years and, as in any other part of the world, often operate with an eye on the short and medium term.

As a large sector, investment in aviation doesn't yield immediate returns. Infrastructure and airplanes are expensive. Governments or private investors generally won't see returns within a year or two; they will need to wait five to ten years. The key factor to remember is, for those who stay the course, the rewards of building a strong aviation sector can be great. Investing in the aviation sector may not yield tangible results within an individual government's term of office, but it will have a positive effect on the country's long-term future. To see the potential of the aviation sector will require leaders to think boldly and commit to a vision of a better, more connected Africa.

CHAPTER TWO

WHY AFRICA MUST FLY TO RISE

Yamoussoukro is a little-known African city in the middle of the savannah. It's also the political and economic capital of Côte d'Ivoire, the home of the country's founding father and first president, Félix Houphouët-Boigny, and, according to the *Guinness Book of Records*, home to the world's largest church. In 1999, forty-four African countries came together in Yamoussoukro to agree on an open-skies policy. Twenty-seven years later, in 2016, the heads of numerous African nations returned to the city to sign the Yamoussoukro Decision, designed to create a framework for liberalizing African aviation. This latest accord was one in a series of declarations signed in the city over the course of more than thirty years.

The intention of the African heads of state who signed the decision was to break down artificial barriers obstructing air transport services, especially between African nations. As yet, however, none of the numerous accords signed in Yamoussoukro have been implemented in any meaningful way. Despite the goodwill they generated and the positive intentions of everyone involved, improvement has been stymied by the real challenges of moving from declaration to implementation.

When the first declaration was signed, the ordinary people of Côte d'Ivoire were largely unaware of its existence. Eric was in high school in Yamoussoukro, yet he, like so many residents of the city, had no knowledge of the event. For the aviation industry, it should have been a monumental moment. To the average Ivorian, however, there was little indication of what was at stake.

Yamoussoukro is a hub of academic activity, containing a number of excellent schools for engineering, agronomy, and the sciences. As of 2017, however, the local airport remains largely unused. Located forty-five minutes from the city, it hosts only one carrier, Air Côte d'Ivoire, and welcomes no more than a handful of arrivals each week. As this book goes to press, there are no scheduled international flights into or out of Yamoussoukro.

During the signing of the most recent accord in May 2016,

leaders of twenty-one African countries committed to five separate resolutions aimed at easing air travel restrictions across the continent. However, not one of those resolutions has been implemented.

This is especially disappointing because allowing non-national airlines to carry passengers between third countries—fifth freedoms—can significantly reduce air fares and increase passenger traffic. Since liberalization in 2003, the route between Nairobi and Johannesburg has seen a sixty-ninefold increase in passenger volume. When routes across the Southern African Development Community (SADC) opened, fares dropped by 18 percent.

The potential benefits of airspace liberalization are large and should be pursued vigorously. Inter*VISTAS* estimated that liberalization between the five East African Community (EAC) countries could result a 41 percent increase in flight frequencies, while lowering fares by 9 percent. This, in turn, could increase passenger traffic by 29 percent.

The tale of the Yamoussoukro Decision is an example of the stagnation that too often besets aviation in Africa. Sadly, it's far from the only example. Around 2010, several economists and global publications sat up and took notice as African growth rates rose to 5 percent. Even well-known pessimists were excited, with many people daring to believe that Africa's time had come.

Unfortunately, a number of factors have subsequently slowed African growth. Falling oil prices have had a huge impact on some of the continent's largest economies, including Nigeria. South Africa, the continent's second largest economy, has been plagued by political fighting and currency fluctuations. Security issues have also played a significant role in disrupting the narrative of African ascendance. The Arab Spring caused economic chaos in Egypt, Tunisia, and Libya, three of Africa's larger economies. Finally, China, one of Africa's primary customers for natural resource, experienced a general economic slowdown. Naturally, this had a knock-on effect on the continent. Taken together, these trends significantly slowed economic growth across Africa.

Between 2010 and 2016, growth rates continent-wide dropped to 3.3 percent per year. While this is considerably lower than the 5.4 percent Africa delivered prior to 2010, it's still significantly higher than many other parts of the world. Additionally, many African countries, including Tanzania, Ghana, Côte d'Ivoire, Ethiopia, Kenya, and even the DRC, have continued to experience growth rates above the mean. Nonetheless, the issues experienced across the continent tempered enthusiasm about Africa's economic rise.

While belief in Africa's growth remains shaky, there are several reasons to believe the continent is finally growing in stability and prosperity. If we exclude those countries affected by the

Arab Spring and oil-dependent economies such as Nigeria and Angola, the growth rate in sub-Saharan Africa is impressive. Countries such as Côte d'Ivoire, Tanzania, Rwanda, and the DRC are among the world's fastest-growing economies. Let's examine the factors that are driving this growth.

THE DECLINING RATE OF CONFLICTS

Conflict is incredibly harmful to growth and disruptive to society as a whole. Within families, conflict affects the functioning of individual people. Across countries, or across an entire continent, their impact can be catastrophic. Over the past fifty years, forty-four of the fifty-four countries in Africa have become mired in some form of armed conflict.

Typically, these are not international wars. Instead, they are confrontations between warring factions within countries, tribes, or regions, which take a heavy toll on economies and weaken the fabric of trust that sustains a society.

In recent years, however, there has been a significant decline in conflict across the continent, nourishing hope that Africa can progress toward long-term stability and, in turn, develop economically.

AN UPSURGE IN DEMOCRATIC TRANSITIONS

The acceptance of democracy leads to peaceful transitions of power and stronger governmental frameworks. This naturally makes investors more comfortable. They rely on political stability because their investments will only pay off over the course of years and decades. Without it, they are unwilling to risk their capital.

To meet the continent's development objectives, African countries must invest at least 3.5 percent of total GDP into infrastructure, of which approximately 10 percent must be funneled into transportation. In the absence of stability, it will surely be impossible to find that level of investment.

In 2016, Ghana made a successful democratic transition of power. Tanzania has also conducted a successful transition, as did Nigeria a few years ago. Côte d'Ivoire is planning for an election in 2020. Peaceful transitions are becoming the new norm in African countries, making them more inviting places to invest. In 2016, in Gambia, the country's long-term dictator, Yahya Jammeh, made a decision to allow democratic elections to take place. When he subsequently rejected the results of that election and tried to remain in power, he faced severe resistance from other West African leaders and was eventually forced to relinquish power. This trend bodes well for the future.

INCREASING URBANIZATION AND THE GROWTH OF THE MIDDLE CLASSES

Another factor shaping Africa's future is the rise of urbanization. More Africans live in urban environments than ever before; by 2035, it's anticipated that 60 percent of the population will live in cities. Unfortunately, current projections suggest that about two-thirds of those people will arrive in cities seeking a better life and find themselves relegated to shantytowns.

African cities are growing larger. Over the next twenty years, at least six will probably evolve into megacities.[6] The most likely candidates are Cairo, Dar es Salaam, Kinshasa, Luanda, Lagos, and Johannesburg. To give you an idea of what constitutes a megacity, one of the defining features is the presence of at least ten thousand air travel passengers per day.

This trend will facilitate economic development and the creation of prosperity, because it will allow for the concentration of employment. Larger cities, such as Nairobi, Addis Ababa, and Abidjan, will also grow stronger. In 2016, consumer and business spending across Africa totaled approximately US$4 trillion, of which $1.4 trillion was household consumption and $2.6 trillion was business expenditure. Based on a growth rate of 3.8 percent per year, household consumption is expected to

---

[6] Mariama Sow, "Foresight Africa 2016: Urbanization in the African Context," *Brookings*, December 30, 2015, https://www.brookings.edu/blog/africa-in-focus/2015/12/30/foresight-africa-2016-urbanization-in-the-african-context/

rise to $2.1 trillion by 2025, with business expenditure at $3.5 trillion. Overall, this will constitute an increase of $1.6 trillion, totaling $5.6 trillion.

The African middle class is often overlooked. As it grows, the demand for aviation services will also grow, expanding business opportunities in the multitude of sectors influenced by the aviation industry. In 2014, 54 percent of international tourists reached their destination by air, contributing US$46 billion to the GDP of African economies. In total, an estimated 5.8 million people are employed in sectors related to tourism.

Globally, the figure is even higher. Tourism supports 292 million jobs—that's one in ten jobs on the planet. This number includes hotels, restaurants, local transportation, and car rental. The World Travel and Tourism Council (WTTC) has published research revealing that the contribution of travel and tourism rose to 10.2 percent of world GDP (US$7.6 trillion) in 2016.[7]

WHAT ARE THE KEYS TO AFRICA'S DEVELOPMENT?

In 2016, the UN established seventeen Sustainable Development Goals (SDGS) aimed at ensuring that global economic growth is funneled into genuine improvements in the quality of people's lives. Michael Gill, the executive director of the Air

---

[7] "Economic Impact Analysis," World Travel and Tourism Council, accessed October 13, 2017, https://www.wttc.org/research/economic-research/economic-impact-analysis/

Transport Action Group, made the point that air transport supports fourteen of those seventeen goals, from creating dignified and well-paid jobs and fostering economic growth to improving education and reducing inequalities.

Worldwide, the number of jobs supported by aviation is expected to grow by more than 99 million over the next two decades, with worldwide GDP generated by these jobs reaching US$5.9 trillion. When well managed and developed sustainably, aviation can be a force for good for years to come.

Across the continent, there are numerous initiatives in place aimed at supporting and augmenting African growth. These range from the AUC's Agenda 2063 to the African Development Bank's High Five and the UN's seventeen SDGs, yet each one recognizes the importance of economic integration and infrastructure development if the continent is to reach its development goals. One of the key aims of Agenda 2063 is to inspire countries to drop air travel restrictions in order to facilitate the movement of goods and people across the continent.

This is already beginning to happen. In mid-2016, Benin decided to scrap all visa requirements for Africans traveling to the West African nation. Benin's president, Patrice Talon, said that the decision was made after seeing the success of Rwanda's initiative. Other countries loosening visa restrictions for Africans include Rwanda, the Seychelles, and Ghana. At the time of writing, South Africa is also considering dropping all visa restrictions for African countries.

Translating all this potential into real prosperity remains a considerable challenge. How can we ensure the average citizen has a quality job? How can we ensure people have opportunities to attend good schools, benefit from quality health care, and have access to essential basic services?

If the aspiration underlying the UN's SDGs is to become a reality, we must find ways to help the average African citizen become much more productive. This means finding ways for people to put their skills and energy to positive use. How can we do that?

Cities have a huge role to play in this process. They provide vastly improved access to a huge range of opportunities, enabling people to acquire skills and connect with important services. For investors, cities also open avenues in which to invest in ways that benefit a large percentage of the population. While urbanization in Africa will undoubtedly present challenges, it also offers enormous potential, especially for young people.

Taken individually, even the largest African economies are tiny on a global scale. Until recently, this has held back the growth of the continent. A potential solution exists, however, in the form of integrating markets. Developing stronger, more transparent links between countries can play a key role in growing individual economies, while simultaneously making it easier to pursue mutually beneficial courses of action.

In an increasingly digital economy, connectivity will also become progressively more important. Smart Africa is an initiative championed by Rwanda that seeks to ensure Africa has access to technology, data, and the mechanisms to change and transform life. For that vision to reach fruition, the technological infrastructure to support it must be in place.

With all the above in mind, what are the real opportunities for aviation in Africa? A study undertaken by IATA found that as many as five million passengers per year are denied the chance to travel between twelve key markets due to unnecessary restrictions, limiting employment and growth.[8] While some of the conditions for growth are favorable, it would be unwise to underestimate the challenges. Decades of economic stagnation and low per capita income in many African countries have resulted in the least developed commercial aviation sector in the world.

Nonetheless, Africa is expected to see an extra two hundred million passengers over the next twenty years, creating a total market of three hundred million passengers annually. According to IATA, if twelve key economies such as Algeria, Ethiopia,

---

8   "Value of Aviation," IATA, accessed October 13, 2017, http://www.iata.org/policy/promoting-aviation/Pages/index.aspx

Ghana, and Uganda opened their skies to one another, fares would drop by 35 percent and an extra five million people could afford to fly.

In pockets of the continent, this approach has already paid dividends. A more liberal air market between South Africa and Kenya in the early 2000s led to a 69 percent rise in passenger traffic. The 2006 Morocco-European Union (EU) open skies agreement led to a 160 percent rise in traffic between the two countries. The operation of a low-cost carrier service between Johannesburg, South Africa, and Lusaka, Zambia, resulted in a 38 percent reduction in fares and a 38 percent increase in passenger traffic. That's particularly significant in the context of a relatively depressed low-cost market. At present, low-cost airlines constitute only 10 percent of the continent's total flights.

THE ROLE OF AVIATION IN ECONOMIC GROWTH

As discussed in the introduction, aviation supports almost every sector of the economy, making it both a direct and an indirect contributor to job creation. Aviation requires skilled and semiskilled labor, meaning that jobs in the sector usually attract talented people and respectable pay. Forecasts indicate that aviation will support roughly one hundred million quality jobs on the continent by 2034, generating US$6 trillion of economic activity. Aviation jobs also produce transferable skills, broadening the horizons of those who work in the sector. A person checking in passengers at the airport in Abidjan can easily transfer that skill to a job in Togo, Benin, or even Paris.

In addition to creating jobs, aviation is also highly profitable. A professional operator running an effective business in the African airline sector can turn a solid profit. Air France flights to Abidjan, for example, are some of the company's most profitable routes. Two Air France planes land in Abidjan every day, some of them A380s, and all of them are almost full. Similarly, British Airways' route between London and two Nigerian cities, Lagos and Abuja, fare extremely well. Route profitability is a closely guarded secret, but industry analysts estimate that both are among British Airways' ten most profitable.

Aviation in Africa is a unique opportunity for profits to match purpose. Investors can see good returns on their investments, while also creating positive results for African people. It's especially satisfying to make money in a way that serves others.

As of 2017, Nigeria's incumbent state minister for aviation, Senator Hadi Abubakar Sirika, clearly understood this relationship. While speaking on the theme of "Driving African Economies through the Power of Aviation" at the IATA African Aviation Day in Abuja, Nigeria, he commented,

> Enhanced air transport connectivity is inarguably the key condition for any state's progress and transportation. Stud-

ies have shown that there is a clear correlation between connectivity and economic performance. In addition, improved connectivity attracts inward investment, which enables access to export markets and opens countries up to competitive forces. Improved connectivity means more access to cities, markets, business, and people, as well as integration into global supply chains, another important factor for attracting inward investment into any country.[9]

The relationship is intuitive. Connectivity contributes to a higher quality of life for Africans and simultaneously attracts more tourists to the continent.

Unfortunately, investment in the African aviation sector is very low in comparison with other continents. In turn, this leads to a lack of trust in African aviation and limited investment. Some travelers, including many investors, aren't willing to fly on airlines with which they aren't familiar, so they won't travel to many parts of Africa. This is especially true in Nigeria, which has a reputation for playing host to some of the most dangerous airlines on the planet.

Additionally, investing in African aviation is a complex proposition. The sector is already complex, and the additional

---

[9] Lawani Mikairu, "Sirika Calls for Enhanced Air Connectivity among African Countries," *Vanguard*, June 6, 2016, https://www.vanguardngr.com/2016/06/sirika-calls-enhanced-air-connectivity-among-african-countries/

bureaucratic and infrastructural hurdles in Africa may deter potential investors. This creates a vicious circle. The difficulty of investment puts people off doing so, and the lack of large investments sends the message that aviation is not a promising sector in which to invest. Nonetheless, most of the biggest fortunes in the world are made in times of crisis. The boldest and most farsighted investors understand that opportunities exist where others fear to tread.

In 2016, the African Development Bank launched the African Regional Integration Index, aimed at revealing the connection levels of different African countries and persuading many to drop barriers to integration. At the time of writing, it's impossible to read the index and not conclude that there's a lot of work to be done before the continent attains this goal.

GREATER INTEGRATION CAN SUPPORT A GREATER SENSE OF BELONGING

An improved aviation sector would have a tremendous positive impact on the country's trade. Some African countries produce items that could find ready markets in the West or in other high-income markets, if only it were possible to transport the goods.

The few countries that have succeeded in doing this have already reaped considerable benefits. Kenya's horticultural industry, for example, has benefited from the country's comparatively developed aviation sector. Ethiopia's massive flower farms are prospering thanks to airlines that move the cargo quickly and in a cost-effective manner. Many other African countries, however, have attempted to compete in those sectors and failed miserably, simply because they didn't have the freight capacity to provide regular, reliable supplies.

Aviation can be a bridge between Africa and the rest of the world, allowing African countries to send high-value goods to markets around the globe. As we write, it's extremely difficult for a farmer in Lilongwe, Malawi, to deliver produce to world markets, severely limiting the growth potential of the sector. Aviation could change that.

Another benefit offered by an improved aviation sector is the ability to import important products more affordably, such as mobile phones and essential medicine. Medicine poses a particular problem, because many medicines must be kept at specific temperatures during shipping, making them expensive to ship. The shorter transportation times of aviation can reduce costs.

Free trade agreements only result in increased trade when they are backed up by mechanisms to translate those agreements into deliverable products. Free trade between China and Africa has flourished because the majority of Africa's most developed airlines are located in eastern Africa. Free trade between the

EU and Africa, on the other hand, has floundered, even though agreements have been in place since the 1980s.

Aviation can become a missing link, using the EU trade agreement to generate real opportunities for exchange. This scenario promises both free movement of goods and increased opportunities for Africans to meet their international counterparts to do business. This approach could even benefit trade between Africa and China. At present, most of the trade derives from natural resources leaving Africa for China and finished goods coming from China to Africa. Improved aviation could play a vital role in facilitating greater interpersonal connection and a more varied business environment.

A thriving aviation sector has the potential to drive economic convergence between Africa and other regions of the world. By doing so, it can make a tangible difference in quality of life. Simultaneously, and just as importantly, it can give African people reason to be proud of their birthplace. As it transports goods and people around the world, aviation has the paradoxical potential to bring people together, as communities prosper and people no longer need to seek a better life for themselves and their families elsewhere in the world.

SECTION TWO

FOUNDATIONS OF AFRICAN AVIATION

CHAPTER THREE

STAKEHOLDERS IN AVIATION

Aviation is a complex industry, with numerous potential pitfalls. A successful aviation sector requires the presence of many engaged stakeholders. In the absence of one or more, the system becomes overtaxed. Many African countries struggle to meet the needs and interests of these myriad stakeholders, leading to an unbalanced sector. This is why it's so important to understand the different stakeholders and their roles in aviation infrastructure.

Most passengers arriving at an airport have only one objective: to board their plane. This singular focus makes them blind to the plethora of companies, processes, systems, and entities that make it possible for an aircraft to take off from one airport and land at another.

Long before passengers reach the airport, for example, most book their tickets via travel agents. Before credit cards were common, travel agents were a necessity. People either paid them in cash or by secured credit. Travel agents then connected them with hotels and airlines. This was especially useful for complex journeys. Imagine a passenger traveling from Kuwait to London, then London to Frankfurt, then from Frankfurt back to Kuwait. Travel agents facilitated this process.

Many people believe that travel agencies are a dying breed, rapidly being replaced by online booking services. Many passengers, however, still prefer to use travel agents to alleviate the complexity of booking several flights at once, especially where entire families are involved. This is especially true in Africa, where not everyone has a credit card.

Most passengers park in airport parking facilities. Those facilities are managed by specialized companies. After parking, passengers typically proceed directly to check-in, a service run by a ground handling business. At its core, Hassan's company (NAS) is a ground handling business. No doubt you're familiar with the routine. Passengers give their bags to an agent at the counter, who also examines the passenger's passport and looks up their records on the computer. The agent then prints out a boarding pass and luggage tags, attaches the tags to the passenger's luggage, and places the luggage on a belt. The luggage is taken somewhere underneath the airport, into a realm where few people have ever ventured.

From there, passengers take their boarding pass to immigration, receiving a stamp to prove that they've left the country. After that, they pass through security. Then, they either go to a lounge to wait for boarding, wander around the duty-free shops, or find a seat somewhere else. An entire industry of companies exists to provide products for duty-free markets. Lounges, too, are managed by professional operators—a service that NAS also provides.

Prior to boarding, bathrooms and aisles are cleaned and water is loaded onto the aircraft. All of these tasks also fall within the remit of Hassan's company. While passengers await boarding, their luggage is being sorted. Once the luggage is sorted, it must be transported to the correct aircraft. This is done by ground handling agents. International regulations require passengers to accompany their luggage on flights, a process that must be monitored closely by IT systems. If a passenger doesn't board their flight, or is off-loaded, their baggage must also be removed. This is to eliminate the possibility of unaccompanied bags, known as "red bags," which are considered a high security risk.

Passengers seated on an aircraft can look out of the windows and watch this process taking place. Few people, however, realize how complex it is. Luggage is loaded into the belly of the aircraft in a specific sequence, according to weight, by trained specialists who ensure that the load is balanced. Besides passenger bags, these specialists also load cargo, which is typically stored by the ground handling company until the time comes. In many places, passengers reach their aircraft by bus. In other cases, they traverse a bridge between the terminal and the plane. This process also requires specialist management.

In addition to the above, catering companies provide the food people will eat on board. These differ from the regular catering companies that supply office events and the like, specializing instead in catering for in-flight consumption. Meanwhile, fueling companies provide jet fuel, and maintenance companies ensure that each aircraft is in good condition and safe to fly. These maintenance companies conduct checks prior to all commercial flights. This means that an engineer must come and examine every single aircraft prior to takeoff.

In most airports, several government agencies are at work. One is customs, which plays a huge role handling the cargo that moves in and out of the airport. Another is immigration. Security services protect the perimeter of the airport and prevent dangerous items, such as guns, bombs, and knives, from being brought onto aircraft. While these services are invisible to most passengers, they perform vital roles.

Equally important is air traffic control. This is composed of the men and women who sit in the control tower near the runway and regulate when planes take off and land, and where each aircraft parks. Air traffic control also manages each country's airspace. Every country has its own sovereign airspace and generates revenue from every flight passing through that airspace. The DRC, being a large country right in the center of Africa, generates a lot of income from aircraft passing through its airspace. Smaller countries on the periphery don't earn as much.

Finally, flight support companies provide services to ad hoc or unscheduled flights. If you decided to take a private jet from Côte d'Ivoire to Egypt, for example, you would hire a flight support company to obtain the proper permits to fly through the airspace of the relevant countries. The flight support company would also arrange for the aircraft to be fueled and handle catering during the flight. Private aviation is common in almost every African airport, and most African airports have terminals dedicated specifically to chartered flights, along with terminals for presidents, heads of state, and their guests.

Beyond all these individual components, each airport must be owned and managed as a complete entity, and each country's aviation sector is subject to specific guidance. Experience has shown that the best way to handle these functions is to contract the airport management to a private company, overseen by a governmental regulatory body.

In Africa, this structure is rarely in place. Côte d'Ivoire is one country that has mastered this arrangement. The airport is managed by a private company named Aeria (La Société Aéroport International d'Abidjan), while a government civil aviation authority is responsible for the smooth running of the sector as a whole. Many countries have succeeded in splitting the operation and regulation of airports, but both operators and regulators are owned by the government. This is true in Kenya, where the Kenya Airports Authority and the Kenya Civil Aviation Authority are both government owned. South Africa operates a similar structure, with the South African Civil Aviation Authority overseeing civil aviation, while the Airports Company South Africa (ACSA) owns and operates nine major airports. The latter is a quasi-governmental body, although only 74.6 percent of the outstanding shares are owned directly by the government of South Africa.

While the airport at Abidjan is managed by a private company, there are also African airports that are both owned and operated privately. Two examples come to mind: Lanseria, which we'll discuss later in this book, and Warri Airport in the western Delta State of Nigeria. Also known as Osubi Airstrip, Warri Airport was built by the oil giant Shell and opened in 1999. Originally, it was intended mainly to serve the company's own needs, along with those of other oil companies—somewhere between 20 and 40 percent of Nigeria's oil production originates in the western Delta State.

In 2015, however, Shell sold the airport to a privately owned Nigerian oil and gas company named Shoreline Energy International. As of 2017, the runway is one of the busiest in Nigeria. The airport is run as a commercial enterprise, and the terminal is professionally managed. It is anticipated that scheduled international flights will soon commence, enabling oil executives and people from the western Nigerian Delta to connect directly to the world.

There are also two primary bodies responsible for the global regulation of aviation: IATA and ICAO. ICAO is a UN agency established in 1944 and based in Montreal, Canada, that works with 191 member states of the UN to administer and govern civil aviation around the world.

IATA is managed by the airlines themselves, with a mission to represent and serve the airline industry. All airlines are members of IATA, as is almost every professional service provider in the aviation sector. Non-airline industries, such as ground handling companies, often feel that IATA lobbies too hard for airlines and not enough for other stakeholders in the sector. Although the organization is meant to represent the entire airline industry, the board is composed primarily of airline companies.

To the average traveler, navigating the process of purchasing tickets, checking in at airports, and boarding flights may appear relatively straightforward. Behind the scenes, however, there is an enormous amount of work taking place to make it possible.

UNLEASHING THE POTENTIAL OF AFRICAN AVIATION

Why do all the different components of aviation matter? To understand the potential of aviation as a tool for driving prosperity, it's important to recognize the massive number of jobs it creates and the huge impact it can make, not only in terms of economic activity but also in people's lives. Aviation is often overlooked as a lever for wealth creation. If we wish to change this picture, it's essential that both policymakers and more general stakeholders comprehend the sector, so they can see and help to unleash its potential.

So many stakeholders are involved in making a trip go smoothly, and yet most travelers never see these people. As a frequent business traveler, Eric always associated time spent at the airport with idleness. One of his stated goals is to be the last person boarding the flight. The first time Eric visited Hassan in Kuwait, however, he got a close look at the underbelly of the airport. Consequently, he finally understood the processes that make an airport work. Seeing them firsthand for the first time was eye-opening.

For every aspect of a journey, there's an organization with a specific mission. Unfortunately, some African countries aren't yet equipped to ensure that all these missions are fulfilled. African airports, for example, may feature government workers pinch-hitting as ground handlers, or private sector operators using their connections to secure preferential deals. With a focus on cronyism instead of service, they may fail to understand the industry and fail to deliver on their commitments. In some African countries, checking baggage is a risky endeavor. Without competent, experienced teams, luggage—or its contents—goes missing far too frequently.

Operating at an airport can be a lucrative niche. Companies can charge passengers in foreign currencies. Due to aviation's status as a luxury for the privileged few, they can demand high prices. As a result, monopolies can emerge. In many instances, concessions are handed out as political favors. A ground handling company, for example, might be rewarded for supporting a specific political candidate.

Unfortunately, this is a common scenario in Africa. Small, local companies, which have won the favor of a powerful politician or are linked to a historic partner, handle functions that should be managed by professional, global companies that can call on best practices, policies, procedures, systems, and expertise. The result is a fragmented, poorly coordinated industry characterized by small companies that care little about brand, reputation, or quality of service. They only want to survive and rake in as much money as they can.

In some African countries, there are airports with poor-quality concessions, or even no concessions at all. This leads to a loss of revenue for governments, who may be oblivious to the amount of money they are losing. NAS, Hassan's company, pays a concession fee to the government in every location where the company operates. The amount is usually calculated as a percentage of revenue, and concessions are awarded through competitive bidding or another transparent process.

Small, local companies that have operated the same concession for ten to twenty years often pay no government royalties whatsoever. This means that the government generates no funds from the presence of these services at the airport. While the government loses revenue from this arrangement, the more profound consequence is that these are funds that could be reinvested in airport infrastructure and the aviation ecosystem.

NATIONAL CARRIERS AND PRIVATE CARRIERS

When many African countries became independent in the 1960s, every one of them wanted to have their own airline. For them, owning an airline was a symbol of sovereignty and branding. It became a way of declaring their prestige to the world.

A flurry of national airlines came into existence during this period, although most of them proved to be white elephants. The airline business is extremely competitive and complex, and many countries struggled to succeed in the unfamiliar environment. Sadly, few of them learned the lessons of those early mistakes. At the time of writing, the vicious circle continues. Countries and individuals found airlines, watch them go bankrupt, and then try again. Sometimes, it seems as though every day heralds the birth of a new national airline, while another dies. As of 2010, twenty-five African carriers were fully or partially owned by governments.

Gradually, however, several trends are emerging that may help African airlines succeed. Several are working with financial institutions such as EXIM Bank, which enables countries to lease new aircraft. The African EXIM Bank, for example, financed Air Côte d'Ivoire's first aircraft, which today flies to more than twenty destinations in West Africa. In addition, development partners are becoming available to fund large infrastructure projects and provide the financing airlines need to grow.

A number of smart and structured private companies, such as fastjet and VIA, are entering the market. Fastjet is a low-cost airline, while VIA is a flight support company. Susan Mashibe, the president and CEO of VIA, is a perfect example of a skilled private operator who is blazing a trail that others can follow. Finally, some national airlines are developing partnerships with global players. KLM and Air France-KLM, for example, now hold shares in Kenya Airways.

In 2016, Hassan met the head of state of a major West African country with a vibrant aviation sector but no national carrier. Hassan congratulated the head of state on rejecting the idea of a national carrier and encouraging other carriers. He was surprised, however, when his companion stated that the country was planning to launch a national carrier and place all airport services, from ground handling to cargo to duty free, under its control. Hassan knew this would be a tragic mistake. Airlines should focus on transporting people and cargo from point A to point B. Other airline services should be left to specialized companies.

With all due respect, Hassan attempted to persuade the head of state to change his mind. He was adamant, however, that he wanted to create a national carrier. The country planned to use government funds for the purpose and had even approached a European airline to offer advice on how to launch. In 2017, Hassan met an adviser of the same head of state and was told that plans for a state carrier have been scrapped. Instead, the country will be focusing on encouraging foreign and local carriers, as Hassan originally advised.

As with any economic activity, there are certain conditions that make founding an aviation business desirable and sustainable. It's the responsibility of any leader—of a government or a company—to assess the predominant market conditions and the potential for success before starting an airline. Aviation can be very profitable when properly managed, but there's also a risk that airlines can become a drain on government coffers. Airline companies are private enterprises, and their objective is to make a profit. They measure success by how much return on investment they can give to their shareholders. Unless they can compete in a global market, we generally discourage governments from starting airlines.

Nonetheless, there are a few exceptions to this rule. Some governments launch airlines not simply because they wish to advertise their sovereignty or national pride, but because they want to put their city on the map, with all the attendant benefits that brings. For Dubai, aviation is an integrated strategy, not a stand-alone investment. By transporting people to and from the city, it has played a key role in transforming Dubai into a regional hub. This mission has been fulfilled, making Emirates a success on its own terms.

The key question for leaders to ask themselves is whether a national carrier meets their long-term objectives. Is the presence of a national carrier part of an integrated strategy? Even in Dubai, the government should still be looking ahead two or three decades and asking whether it will still make financial sense to support the country's airline.

This question is equally relevant for Côte d'Ivoire. The government wants to create a West African hub and has chosen to support Air Côte d'Ivoire financially as part of this project. This may seem like a good approach at present, but what will happen as Air Côte d'Ivoire grows? Will it become self-sustaining, or will the government find itself propping up an increasingly unsustainable airline? The airline's original capital was twenty-five billion Ivorian francs—about US$40 million. This was increased to sixty-five billion Ivorian francs in 2016, and again to two hundred billion in 2017. Air France-KLM, which owns 20 percent of the airline, participated in the capital increase, indicating that they believe it's a good investment.

Another reason why many governments are motivated to create national carriers is to serve routes that would otherwise be neglected. In Côte d'Ivoire, for example, foreign carriers will happily fly into Abidjan but have little interest in serving smaller Ivorian cities such as San Pedro. Governments may want these routes to be effectively served to sustain national unity, serve businesspeople, allow students to travel to university, or help patients reach major cities to receive medical treatment. This is a noble intention, aimed at easing the difficulties of travel by road.

But however positive the motive, there is reason to be cautious about this approach. As urbanization increases the size of Africa's largest cities, a few vast urban centers are attracting huge numbers of people, while secondary centers are growing more slowly. It's important that governments understand projected demand and align their investments and assets with areas of greatest need. Governments can also decide to grant landing rights to airlines at their preferred destinations, on the condition that they also fly to underserved cities. If airlines want to fly to Jeddah or Riyadh in Saudi Arabia, for example, they are usually required to serve lesser-known cities. A similar principle operates in India.

When governments fail to understand demand, they make consistent mistakes. One is the acquisition of aircraft that are too small to travel internationally, yet too large to effectively serve routes between a capital city and smaller urban centers. This leads to unnecessarily high ticket prices, making it even harder to run airlines at or close to capacity. In Côte d'Ivoire, a ticket between Abidjan and San Pedro costs around US$100. For the average citizen, this isn't a realistic expenditure.

Ghana demonstrates a more successful approach. Many of the country's remote cities are connected by commercial airlines such as Starbow, founded by private investors, and Africa World Airlines, which is owned by China's Hainan Airlines. As commercial entities, they are better equipped to respond to demand, meaning that they can assign aircrafts of an appropriate size to the relevant routes. They are also more effectively governed.

Although Starbow has been rebranded several times since it was founded in 1997, it still serves Kumasi, Takoradi, and Tamale, the three largest Ghanaian cities after the capital Accra. Starbow briefly considered flying some international routes and for a while served Benin and Côte d'Ivoire with some success.

In summary, governments may believe that running national carriers is the only way to maintain national unity, connect remote cities, and simultaneously develop their prestige on the world stage. For all the reasons described above, however, this is rarely a wise investment. Private companies can usually manage airlines more effectively, delivering better services and preventing tax revenues from being funneled toward subsidizing bloated or poorly managed carriers. Governments that recognize this reality are more well-placed for success than those who don't.

SAFETY IN AFRICAN AVIATION

This chapter wouldn't be complete without a discussion of airline safety in Africa. Airlines operating within Nigeria, for example, operate some of the oldest commercial aircraft in the world. They're prone to malfunctions, the air conditioners may leak water, and certain components have been known to give off smoke. These might seem like reasons to be concerned, and they are. In 2004, Africa accounted for one-fifth of all aircraft accidents worldwide, despite the fact that only about 2 percent of global flights passed through the continent. In 2011, the average number of air traffic accidents in Africa was nine times higher than the global average. One of the issues is that, unlike more developed regions, safety regulations are not applied stringently and uniformly. For trust in African airlines to develop, this must change.

Tony Tyler, former director general and CEO of IATA, comments that aviation safety in Africa is moving in the right direction. In fact, according to IATA's 2015 safety report, it's one of the fastest improving regions in the world. To 2010, the five-year average was eleven accidents per year across the continent, with sixty fatalities. Fifty percent of those accidents were attributed to regulatory oversight and 30 percent to airport facilities. In 2015, Africa had eight aircraft accidents, causing thirty-seven fatalities. In 2016, for the first time in a decade, sub-Saharan Africa recorded zero passenger fatalities and jet hull losses.

For public confidence in air travel across the continent to continue to increase, so must levels of safety. The DRC is a poignant example of the challenges faced by African aviation. The country occupies a strategic geographic location within the center of Africa. However, its airspace is badly under-resourced and short of investment. Pilots flying across the country's airspace often complain of poor communications and radar visibility. This translates into a poor safety record, and it is calculated that around half of Africa's aviation-related incidents take place in the DRC or its airspace.

WORKING TOGETHER IS KEY TO THE DEVELOPMENT OF AFRICAN AVIATION

As the old maxim goes: The word *team* stands for "Together Everyone Achieves More." We hope this chapter has shown that there are a huge range of stakeholders directly affected by the quality of the aviation industry. This is even before the multitude of indirect stakeholders is considered. To achieve more, it's essential that major players in the industry understand the roles and responsibilities of each member of the team.

This is especially true of governments, who have a uniquely valuable role to play by supporting private investment and recognizing where government oversight is valuable and where it creates difficulties. For African aviation to grow more sustainable, a free, thriving, and transparent private sector is essential. Each stakeholder has their own perspective and their own expertise. The future of aviation on the continent depends on these divergent entities recognizing their common interests and working together.

CHAPTER FOUR

ONE AFRICA, MANY NATIONS

Africa is one continent, but it contains many diverse nations. To make it easier to think about the different challenges faced by different regions and countries, we'll divide the African continent into four segments and discuss the varying states of aviation development in each one.

SEGMENT ONE: CONTINENTAL HUBS

First, we'll look at what we call the continental hubs. These are countries with one or more hubs, a national airline, and major carriers flying internationally. This segment contains just five countries: Egypt, Ethiopia, Kenya, Morocco, and South Africa. Specifically, the cities where aviation is most concentrated are Cairo, Addis Ababa, Nairobi, Casablanca, and Johannesburg.

Of these countries, three of them—South Africa, Kenya, and Ethiopia—represent 36 percent of international traffic into Africa. Looking at the national carriers individually, South African Airways represents 33 percent of travel to South Africa, Kenya Airways represents 70 percent of travel to Kenya, and Ethiopian represents 83 percent of travel into Addis Ababa.

Transforming these cities into hubs has taken much investment and work. While they are important on a regional level, however, not one features among the dozen most connected global aviation hubs.

It's also interesting to note that there is no meaningful correlation between GDP and the presence of aviation hubs. Africa's largest, richest countries aren't necessarily the ones that play host to the most important hubs. Ethiopia, for example, is a poor country; yet, since independence, it has succeeded in building a thriving aviation sector.

While there are several major hubs in East Africa, there are none of comparable size in sub-Saharan West Africa. Abidjan and Dakar are vying to fill this role, but at present both are too small even to serve as backup hubs for the rest of the continent.

Let's look more closely at Addis Ababa. Currently, this city's airport can handle seven million passengers annually. To expand the country's aviation sector, the government is pursuing two major initiatives: first, the expansion of the existing Bole International Airport; second, a brand-new airport outside Addis Ababa. The government's objective for the new airport is for it to handle seventy million passengers annually. To give you a sense of the scale involved, compare this number with the United Kingdom's premier airport, London Heathrow, which handled seventy-five million passengers in 2015.

The new airport will cost approximately US$3 billion and take eight years to build. The government wishes to do far more than facilitate travel, with plans to create an airport city. The city will feature shopping malls, hotels, an exhibition center, office space, and even residential complexes. In the meantime, expansion of Bole International Airport will cost $250 million and reach completion in 2018, bringing the airport's capacity to twenty million passengers annually. As these initiatives demonstrate, the Ethiopian government is consistent and serious in its commitment to developing the country's aviation sector.

Nonetheless, it would be a mistake to assume that aviation in Ethiopia is perfect. For example, one area for potential improvement is passenger experience. As of 2017, Skytrax rates passenger experience in Bole at three out of ten.[10] The new

---

[10] "Addis Ababa Airport Customer Reviews," Skytrax, accessed October 13, 2017, http://www.airlinequality.com/airport-reviews/addis-ababa-airport/

airport and the expansion of the existing site are intended in part to address these shortcomings.

Nairobi has benefited from its geographic location, along with its reputation as a tourist destination. Situated in a region that gives the country easy access both to the rest of Africa and much of Asia, it has found a ready market for aviation services. The vibrancy of the local Kenyan economy also supports the aviation sector, because other industries, such as horticulture and tourism, utilize aviation services. This boosts demand and further bolsters what is already one of the best-performing economies in East Africa.

Overall, Africa's continental hubs have a lot in common. Each is situated in a location where they have the potential to reach valuable markets in Europe or Asia. Each benefits from strong regulation and investment. Despite our reservations about national carriers, however, all the major African hubs operate a national carrier. We see this as a product of an era when developing a national carrier was often perceived as an essential part of meeting transportation needs. The commercial airline sector lacked the vibrancy we see today. With national carriers held to the same standards as any other commercial endeavor, governments should think carefully about the business case before founding national carriers.

SEGMENT TWO: EMERGING STARS

In addition to the continental hubs, there are numerous countries in Africa that realize the importance of aviation and have already taken steps to develop their aviation sectors. We'll call these the *emerging stars*, and they deserve to be noted and encouraged. While it can be hard to define exactly which countries fit where, we've identified twenty-five countries we would place in this category. In this section, we'll discuss how emerging stars can progress toward the creation of a vibrant aviation sector and describe some examples.

First, it's important for countries wishing to improve their aviation to achieve political stability and a solid trajectory of economic growth. This drives private sector activity. Second, these countries need fair, transparent competition between carriers. To achieve this, governments must be willing to create a level playing field for bids. This allows companies wishing to deliver quality services to prosper, while limiting the opportunities for concessions to be awarded as political favors. The majority of these countries require upgrades in airport infrastructure, along with the instigation of regulations that help airports to function effectively. This is important, both for passengers and cargo traffic. If customs services, for example, don't function effectively, it's difficult for airports to play a significant role in trade.

Côte d'Ivoire is an excellent example of what's possible when a government chooses to support their country's aviation sector. Developing its aviation sector is part of the Ivorian government's strategy to facilitate the country's recovery from past conflict. As such, the government runs a competitive bidding process that has resulted in significant upgrades to the airport in Abidjan. Meanwhile, regulatory bodies have put in place guidelines that have significantly improved the quality of essential services. The fruits of this approach are already visible. Air France recently started flying the Airbus A380 to Abidjan, only the second destination on the continent the company chose to serve using the super jumbo jet.

Rwanda is another country betting on aviation. Leaders of this landlocked nation see an aviation sector as an important way to increase trade linkage and reinforce tourism, the nation's first foreign exchange earner. One of the first actions of President Kagame's new term was breaking ground at the site of the country's $800 million Bugesera International Airport. RwandAir, Rwanda's national carrier, is now serving thirty destinations, including Brussels, London Gatwick, and many West African cities. The country has even signed an agreement with Benin for the two countries to start a new airline together.

Other emerging stars include Tanzania, Ghana, Senegal, Uganda, and Angola. Each country is taking steps to develop a successful aviation sector. Nonetheless, these countries don't carry as much weight as the continental hubs, a factor that can stunt their growth. Existing hubs may seek to outcompete emerging stars, putting a lot of pressure on them and making it hard for them to develop. This is particularly true for Rwanda, which is attempting to build a hub in East Africa. The country is relatively close to Kenya and Ethiopia, both existing hubs. This makes it more challenging to establish a new hub, although the situation may change as overall demand increases.

SEGMENT THREE: TRADITIONAL PLAYERS

A further twenty African countries, in our view, qualify as *traditional players*. These countries suffer from the imposition of aviation models that need to be upgraded if they are to serve people more effectively. Some of these countries have invested heavily in airport infrastructure but haven't succeeded in developing airlines with the capacity to carry a commensurate number of passengers. Others host an airline that is making a huge effort to grow sustainably but lack other vital services. In some instances, imbalances stem from key players or stakeholders taking on responsibilities beyond their sphere of expertise and succumbing to "mission creep." To transcend these limitations, these countries need to consider the entire aviation ecosystem and develop integrated economic strategies. Only when they succeed in diagnosing the problems they face will they be able to begin moving forward.

It's important to stress that there are several factors influencing the development of aviation. There is no shame for a country in being classified as a traditional player. In fact, recognizing that part of the structure of a viable aviation sector is missing can be a vital first step in remedying the deficiency.

An example of a traditional player comes in the form of Swaziland. The king of Swaziland decreed that the country should make a billion-dollar investment in a brand-new airport, King Mswati III International Airport. Swaziland is a small country with a population of only 1.5 million people. Unemployment in the country is presently running at 40 percent. Swaziland has one of the highest poverty rates in the world, along with one of the lowest per capita GDPs. Naturally, most of the country's citizens can't conceive of paying for air travel.

On top of this, Swaziland is close to South Africa. People wishing to travel to and from the country can easily drive to South African airports, where the flights are far more numerous. During the construction process, progress stalled on several occasions, causing costs to double and then triple. Now the airport is finally completed, the country's national carrier, Swaziland Airlink, operates only a single flight per day to South Africa. In a country with the poverty and geographic location of Swaziland, a billion-dollar airport represents a huge waste of government resources on a project with little value for the citizenry.

SEGMENT FOUR: COUNTRIES WITHOUT AVIATION

A few African nations are completely *without aviation*. This is our fourth and final category, and it consists of countries that are too small or too poor to have any kind of aviation sector, or those whose governments have little interest in developing the industry. Lesotho, for example, is surrounded by South Africa. The smaller country depends on its much larger neighbor to meet almost every essential need. As a result, aviation in Lesotho is practically nonexistent. Several other African nations are in a similar position. They have no aviation sector to speak of and no plans to invest in creating one.

WHY IS THERE SO MUCH DISPARITY IN THE AFRICAN AVIATION SECTOR?

Aside from the natural advantages and disadvantages discussed earlier in the chapter, a major reason for the disparities in aviation across Africa is government policy. Governments that have succeeded in nurturing a robust aviation sector are those that are clear about what they want to achieve and how they can get there. They have created clear governance structures to facilitate this process.

This doesn't necessarily mean launching a national carrier. Some successful countries, such as Ghana and Uganda, don't operate government carriers. Yet, their aviation sectors are vibrant and dynamic. On the other hand, countries such as

Ethiopia and Côte d'Ivoire do have national carriers. Despite their different approaches, these four countries share a common clarity about the value of aviation to their economies and a willingness to support the sector.

The governments of Uganda and Ghana have made it clear that they don't wish to create national carriers and won't attempt to do so. Instead, they embrace an open skies policy. This means that they invite every airline in the world to serve their countries, attracting them with a promise of fair and equal treatment.

Ethiopia, of course, has run a national carrier for decades. Yet, the country shares with Ghana and Uganda a clear sense of mission and a solid governance structure. Ethiopian Airlines is not merely an extension of the government. It is shielded from politics and treated as an independent entity; it has a board with a clear mandate. Nor is it a tool to achieve political ends, as are the national carriers in South Africa and Kenya, where infighting and politics often spill over into arguments about airline policy.

Air Côte d'Ivoire enjoys a similar situation. Representatives from Air France-KLM, the Ministry of Transport in Côte d'Ivoire, and the private sector all sit on the company's board. This diversity of opinion and experienced guidance allows it to provide services to its passengers, build a strong reputation in West Africa, and catalyze growth.

Another factor driving disparities is the unrealistic expectations some African countries have of their place on the aviation map. Swaziland illustrates this perfectly. It's unlikely that the country will ever be a geographic hub, due to its location and its small population. The same is true of many other African countries. Political leaders may want their countries to become the next Dubai, but is this a sensible ambition? In conversation with African leaders, we've heard almost all of them express the desire to host an aviation hub. Yet, there are certain preconditions for the establishment of a viable hub. Countries need the vibrancy that comes with successful industries and tourism sectors. Until these are in place, there's a good chance that hubs won't become successful.

Some countries pursue these ambitions despite being landlocked. This makes it especially difficult for them to become hubs. Many thriving international airports, such as Dubai, are situated on or near coastlines. Other countries have an advantage because of a large tourism industry or other thriving industries that create natural demand for aviation.

As with many rules, however, there is the occasional exception. Rwanda is not located favorably for aviation. It's a small, landlocked country, close to Kenya and Ethiopia, homes to two of the most highly developed aviation sectors on the continent. Nonetheless, since the 1994 genocide, Rwanda has worked hard to position itself as an excellent place to do business. Visas, for example, can easily be procured on arrival, meaning that people can quickly form business partnerships. While there's still much work to be done before Rwanda creates a truly thriving aviation sector, there is a real chance that it will succeed. If it does, it will be *despite* the country's natural disadvantages.

The reasons countries or regions evolve into hubs are many and varied. Dubai was conceived as a place for everyone from the Middle East to enjoy themselves, with shopping centers and other tourist activities. To achieve this goal, the ruler of Dubai developed a coherent strategy to grow Dubai from a small port city into an economic powerhouse, aggressively pursuing the development of an aviation sector. The city has become both a financial hub and a place where people can experience the perks of Western living without traveling to Europe or the United States.

New York's John F. Kennedy International Airport, by contrast, has traveled a very different path to hub status. As the city has grown to become one of the world's greatest, the airport has naturally grown to serve more and more visitors, eager to explore the historical and commercial significance of New York or transit into the United States.

The issue for many African countries is understanding how aviation can meet their real needs. They may look to other countries as an example of what they should be aiming to emulate, perhaps unaware of the differences between themselves and those countries. Many smaller countries, for example, want to become the next Ethiopia. This is despite Ethiopia's sixty-year head start in the aviation sector. The country is already home to a huge airport and several aviation schools and has formed successful partnerships with manufacturers. It makes no sense for any other country to try and walk the same path.

African countries that wish to improve their aviation sectors should start by thinking deeply about the real ways in which aviation can serve their citizens and focus on making a difference to people's lives through job creation and fostering the industries that will increase GDP. When they take this approach, they may be able to address the disparities across the continent.

Some countries have suffered recent conflicts, severe droughts, or other serious problems that have undermined their ability to grow economically. Without stability and growth, they are poorly placed to support aviation. Prior to the civil war in Côte d'Ivoire, between 1998 and 2000, the airport in Abidjan served an average of 1.3 million passengers per year. From the beginning of the civil war until 2011, passenger numbers dropped to about six hundred thousand per year. When the war ended, it took five years for passenger numbers to return to prewar levels.

Finally, it's important to mention that international airlines have a huge impact on aviation policy in Africa. In the countries where they operate, British Airways, Air France, and KLM wield a significant influence on national aviation policies.

Before the outbreak of Ebola in Liberia in February 2014, the country had a thriving aviation sector. It hosted regular flights to the United States—via Delta—and London—via British Airways, SN Brussels, Air France, and KLM. When the Ebola crisis erupted, however, almost all of these airlines discontinued flights. Other West African neighbors closed their borders, making the importation of medicines, treatment tents, and other necessities virtually impossible. Nonetheless, President Barack Obama pledged four thousand soldiers to help; many international aid agencies rushed to assist; and local companies, such as Global Logistics Services, which won many accolades from the UN, came together to fight the epidemic.

All told, the virus killed about five thousand people in Liberia alone. After the outbreak, President Ellen Johnson Sirleaf invested in a brand-new passenger terminal at Roberts International Airport. Under the leadership of Liberia Airport Authority chairman Gbehzongar Findley and CEO Wil Bako Freeman, Liberia has been able to attract back at least some of the foreign carriers that stopped flights earlier due to Ebola.

Some might argue that Liberia stands as an example of the need for a national carrier, as commercial carriers pulled out of the country when Ebola struck. It should be remembered, however, that outbreaks such as Ebola are the exception, not the rule. Other countries wouldn't have allowed any flights from Liberia to land, via a national carrier or otherwise. In other words, the presence of a national carrier wouldn't have eased Liberia's troubles in this instance.

THE FUTURE OF AFRICAN HUBS

As discussed above, North Africa and East Africa contain most of the continent's major hubs. Many parts of West Africa and Central Africa, on the other hand, have experienced sharp declines since 2001. Since then, growth has been small, or even negative.

The reasons for the emergence of existing hubs have already been described: strong governance, the development of effective ancillary services, and ongoing investment in human capital. Africa's existing hubs all host dominant, state-owned carriers, although we don't see this as an essential component of success. Most of the aviation academies are, understandably, also located in these countries.

Perhaps the most prominent African hub is Addis Ababa. Despite being landlocked, it is ideally located in the center of East Africa and has benefited from years of government support and investment. There's nothing to suggest that this situation will change in the foreseeable future.

Cairo's location, on a nexus between Europe and Africa, has also made it an ideal hub. This has been reinforced by the fact that Egypt is a major tourist destination. The country is home to eighty million people and a huge tourism sector. As the world's most populous Arab country, there are many people wishing to visit. Sadly, the aftermath of the 2011 Arab Spring, coupled with the evaluation of the Egyptian pound, has placed the aviation sector in Egypt under threat. In addition, three recent incidents involving the country, including one fatal crash of an EgyptAir jet, have also harmed Egypt's aviation prospects.

If Egypt fails to recover, Casablanca in Morocco is poised to take Cairo's place. The country's national carrier, Royal Air Maroc, is growing steadily, and the king of Morocco has laid out a very clear aviation policy. Realizing the importance of thriving airports for tourism, exports, and connecting Morocco to the rest of Africa and Europe, he has made development of the country's eleven major airports a cornerstone of his economic policy.

Politically, Morocco is well situated. It's an Arab country, so it has a link to the Arab world. It's also an African country, so it has deep connections to the dynamism of Africa. Additionally, it's Europe's neighbor, and its people speak fluent French as well as Arabic, so it has deep ties to Europe.

By positioning the country as a connecting point between these three different civilizations, the king of Morocco is leveraging his nation's natural advantages. Morocco recently rejoined the AU. Previously, that tie was severed due to disagreements over Western Sahara, but Morocco has finally reached an agreement with the AU to resolve the situation. The country's airports are efficiently run by the Office National des Aéroports, established in 1990. While this body is part of the state, it is quasi-independent and led by a seasoned aviation executive, Zouhair El Aoufir, and his team. They manage all of Morocco's airports, including Casablanca, which handles 40 percent of the country's aviation traffic, and Marrakesh, which handles 15 percent. If Morocco's aviation sector continues to grow while Egypt's declines, Casablanca could overtake Cairo as a major hub in the coming years.

Johannesburg's emergence as a hub is built largely on tourism and local demand. South Africa's status as the largest economy on the continent means that a comparatively large number of its citizens can afford to fly. This could change, however. Political conflicts within South Africa have affected South African Airways, making it vulnerable to bankruptcy. To retain its status as a hub, Johannesburg must privatize South African Airways, create an aviation city at the airport, and invest more heavily in essential services. Otherwise, it may fade.

In West Africa, where hubs are smaller and less developed, several cities are emerging as potential aviation centers. Accra in Ghana competes with Abidjan and, to a lesser extent, Lagos in Nigeria and Dakar in Senegal. As described above, Abidjan is doing well, supported by clear direction from the Ivorian government, along with significant government investments in both the national carrier and the aerocity that is under construction within the airport. In addition, the African Development Bank, which moved its headquarters from Abidjan to Tunisia when the Ivorian civil war broke out, has moved its head office back to Abidjan. While Abidjan is progressing well, however, Accra and Lagos both have one natural advantage: in both countries, English is the primary language. Operating without national carriers, it remains to be seen whether their open skies policies will allow them to overtake Côte d'Ivoire.

The airport at Dakar is one of the oldest in West Africa. Although it hasn't been well maintained, in 2011 the country's government secured US$555 million from the African Development Bank, the French bank BNP Paribas, the French Development Agency, and other sources, with the intention of building a new airport. In 2015, the newly elected president of Senegal, Macky Sall, stated publicly that he was unhappy with the lack of progress made in the construction of the new airport by the Saudi Binladin Group. In light of his dissatisfaction, he awarded construction, management, and operation of the airport to two Turkish companies, Summa and Limak. The project is expected to reach completion in 2017.

Ultimately, aviation hubs are economic hubs. They emerge in specific places for specific economic reasons, and they cannot be willed into existence in wholly unpromising environments, purely to serve the ambitions of political leaders. Those hubs that are thriving are supported by stable governments and currencies. They exist in cities where tourists feel safe, where the carriers have strong safety records, and where there is good connectivity with other cities. Flexible visa policies also aid the creation and development of hubs.

Stable governments shield aviation stakeholders from political infighting, protecting their investments. National carriers aren't essential, but there must be a way for feeder airlines from the region to bring passengers into the hub, enabling long-haul carriers to transport them to destinations further afield.

In 2017, Africa probably doesn't need more hubs. With the trends toward urbanization, population growth, and economic integration, however, coupled with developments in technology, the potential for growth in the aviation sector is huge. Could some African countries develop aviation hubs? It's possible. The more pressing need, however, is for the increased sophistication of existing hubs. As the next section of this book will show, there are huge opportunities for entrepreneurs wishing to provide higher-quality services at existing airports.

SECTION THREE

OPPORTUNITIES IN AVIATION IN AFRICA

CHAPTER FIVE

UPGRADING AVIATION INFRASTRUCTURE

As noted in the UN's SDGs, there's a lot of evidence to show that providing access to basic infrastructure has an important role to play in increasing the productivity of developing countries, in all sectors. Aviation is no exception to this rule, and infrastructure is arguably the biggest investment opportunity in African aviation.

Lanseria International Airport was founded in 1972 by two South African pilots, after the municipality purchased the land and rented it to the Lanseria Management Company on a ninety-nine-year lease. Initially, it was no more than a grass strip located northwest of Johannesburg. As an interesting point of trivia, when Nelson Mandela was released from prison in 1990, his journey to Johannesburg took him through Lanseria.

In 2012, the airport was sold to a consortium of private players, including an infrastructure development fund, a women's empowerment company, pension funds, and a public investment corporation. These interests invested in the infrastructure and reopened the airport, making it a busy hub for private jets and other ad hoc flights. Lanseria even hosts some commercial flights, from operators such as Mango and FlySafair. In fact, it's now the fourth busiest South African airport, making it an intriguing example of a thriving African enterprise and a rare instance of a privately owned and operated airport in Africa.

On the other end of the spectrum lies Lilongwe, the capital of Malawi. Malawi is a tiny, landlocked country with a population of more than twenty million people and one of the lowest GDPs per capita in the world. In 2010, Hassan toured the airport in Lilongwe. Once a week, an Emirates flight from Dubai landed in Lilongwe, and he noticed that it always arrived with a full cargo of electronics, medicine, and food, yet left completely empty.

Through conversations with community leaders, Hassan subsequently discovered that although Lilongwe has a vibrant horticultural industry, it has no access to international markets. He reminded them that every week, an Emirates flight departed the airport completely empty. Surely it was a perfect opportunity to export some of Malawi's horticultural produce to the wider world.

In the same way as there are multiple players in the entire aviation sector, however, there are also multiple players in individual airports. Sometimes they don't communicate effectively with one other, or the lack of one has an impact on others. In this case, Hassan was informed that the lack of X-ray machines at the airport made it impossible to transport produce via Malawi. Because outgoing cargo couldn't be x-rayed, international regulations prevented Malawi's valuable horticultural produce from being loaded onto the plane.

In infrastructural terms, X-ray machines aren't especially expensive compared with the value they create. High-quality machines can be purchased for half a million dollars. Unfortunately for Lilongwe, the absence of this critical piece of infrastructure is undermining the economic impact the airport could have on the economy. Is it government bureaucracy, inappropriate decision making, poor budgeting, or a combination of the three that place the X-ray out of reach for the airport? Hassan knew that if the airport was managed by a private company, resources would be found to purchase an X-ray machine. No manager worth their salt would miss the opportunity to utilize an existing empty aircraft to export Malawi's produce, creating a win-win scenario for the airlines, the community, and the international customers who could benefit from receiving the produce.

THE IMPORTANCE OF INFRASTRUCTURE INVESTMENT

As the above examples demonstrate, the private sector has a great deal to offer African aviation. Most people see airports simply as runways, with airplanes taking off and landing, but in reality, building an airport takes a heavy investment of time, money, and resources. Airports need parking facilities, terminals, cargo warehouses, a control tower, an apron on which to park aircraft, and much more. An airport is a complex and expensive ecosystem. For investors, it takes years before they see the results of their commitment. It also takes the right vision, strategy, and skills to invest in infrastructure today for current and future demands. Airports are no exception.

Sadly, African aviation infrastructure lags far behind infrastructure in the rest of the world. Compounding the problem, the investment that *does* take place often isn't aligned with the stated ambitions of African countries. Yet, well-developed infrastructure supports productivity, enables tourism, and boosts economic activity. It's also a necessity for the provision of basic services.

This aviation infrastructure challenge is part of a broader

strategic issue for Africa. Investment in infrastructure across Africa, as a percentage of GDP, is still low. The numbers are much smaller than, for example, the Asian Tigers (Hong Kong, Singapore, South Korea, and Taiwan) during their periods of accelerated growth. In 2009, the International Monetary Fund estimated that Africa would invest a total of 24 percent of GDP into all types of infrastructure. While this may sound like a lot, it's much less than the 40 percent invested by the Asian Tigers at their peak. The Centre for Aviation (CAPA) has estimated that US$34 billion is currently earmarked for airport construction in seventy-seven projects across Africa. These projects include $2.1 billion for Tripoli, $952 million for Algiers, $800 million for Bugesera (the new airport near Kigali), and $500 million for Lusaka. Again, these numbers may seem impressive. Compare them with the Middle East, however, where $53 billion has been invested across a much smaller landmass to bring the industry to its current state, and you'll see the disparity.

In addition, the Middle East is already far more developed than Africa, so Africa needs to spend more if it is even to begin closing the gap. In Europe, another developed region, current investment in airport construction is touching US$100 billion. If African nations wish to take aviation seriously and meet stated development objectives, they have a lot of work to do.

It's true that spending on aviation infrastructure in Africa has more than doubled, from an average of $36 billion per year between 2001 and 2006 to $80 billion in 2015. Yet, this still represents only about 3.5 percent of GDP. According to the McKinsey Global Institute report *Lions on the Move II*, annual infrastructure investment needs to double to $150 billion by 2025 if African infrastructure is to adequately support the continent's economic development. To make this possible, governments must develop bankable projects, ensure adequate financing, put in place effective public-private partnerships, and optimize spending.

It's reasonable to wonder why African infrastructure has not already undergone adequate improvements. To understand, let's investigate the contributing factors. First, African governments have limited resources and competing priorities, which often lead them to make trade-offs and compromises. In countries where suitable land is limited, aviation may be pushed down the list of priorities. This is especially true of countries where there's a general belief that aviation is only for the wealthy or privileged.

Many aviation infrastructure projects could be facilitated with stronger public-private partnership (PPP) framework. In order for such PPP mechanisms to succeed, however, effective governance mechanisms must be in place. Laws that will make investment appealing must be established. Major players often shy away from Africa due to corruption or a perception of corruption, which makes it difficult to create transparent frameworks for PPP. International investors—foundations, institutions, and nongovernmental organizations—may want to invest in infrastructure projects, but they end up navigating opaque bidding processes or negotiating with inexperienced people. This makes the whole process cumbersome and unappealing.

To address this situation, African leaders and governments must create simple PPP frameworks for investors that will protect all parties for the ten, fifteen, or twenty years necessary to upgrade infrastructure. Development partners must also step in to provide support, because many African governments are not capable of providing their share of funding without partners such as the World Bank, International Finance Corporation, Department for International Development, and the Chinese.

The final factor is the presence of skilled people who wish to invest their energies in a better Africa. The continent has difficulty keeping hold of its best and brightest. They may be tempted by higher-paying, more secure roles elsewhere. Given the right conditions, however, they will surely choose to play a role in helping their homes to thrive.

IS THE SITUATION IMPROVING?

The DRC is the largest country in sub-Saharan Africa. Traveling through the country, whether over land or by air, is very challenging. This is due to a combination of factors: poor road infrastructure, conflicts, neglect, underinvestment, the breakdown of law and order, and other issues. Goma International Airport, located in the eastern part of the DRC, serves as the international gateway for that part of the country. Unfortunately, the problems listed above have contributed to its poor condition.

The most significant damage to the airport, however, stems from the volcanic eruption of Mount Nyiragongo in 2002. Eric was an unlikely witness to this event as he was a mere thirty kilometers from Goma the day of the eruption. The lava flow buried about a third of the runway, isolating the terminal and apron. This impacted humanitarian and UN flights into the country, exacerbating the DRC's other problems in the country.

The Goma Airport Safety Improvement Project is an initiative aimed at addressing the situation. Funded by the World Bank, it provides a US$52 million grant for the reestablishment of safe and secure operations at Goma International Airport, with the objective of breaking the DRC's isolation. This grant comes on the heels of a German grant provided in 2009, along with several others, all with the intention of fixing this problem. The plan is to rehabilitate the existing runway and apron, revive the control tower, rebuild the destroyed security fence around the airport, and restore the cargo warehouse and passenger terminal.

The Goma Airport Safety Improvement Project is only one of

several projects aimed at lifting African aviation infrastructure to a higher standard. It serves both as an example of how infrastructure investment can be effective and an indication that perhaps the tide is turning.

Travel around Africa and you will see a number of new terminals being built. You may also notice land being opened up for aviation development, along with improvements to existing infrastructure in process. Slowly, the situation is improving, and the continent may be on the verge of an inflection point. African aviation may yet be a long way from where it needs to be to raise the living standards of the continent, but there are green shoots. We're moving in the right direction.

CHAPTER SIX

AVIATION SUPPORT SERVICES IN AFRICA

What are support services and why do they matter? Aviation support services include every service in airports but airlines themselves—from managing parking facilities and lounges to ground handling, check-in, the management of bags and cargo, aircraft cleaning, and busing passengers. Beyond direct services to airlines, ancillary services such as catering companies and duty-free companies also fall under the category of aviation support services.

Each of these support services contributes to the comfort of passengers and effective movement of cargo throughout their journey. They provide passengers with clean, comfortable lounges, ensure that bags are waiting on arrival, and contribute to safety and security. Few people realize that it's essential for bags and cargo to be loaded and balanced properly in the belly of the aircraft. Improperly loaded aircraft are harder to fly; on occasion, they have crashed.

In addition, companies wishing to import medicine, fruits and vegetables, or fish must store them at a specific temperature and ensure that they're handled safely. Rules are in place to prevent medicine from being tampered with. Each of these tasks requires the skills and hard work of support services.

Support services carry a low profile in comparison with airlines, but they are responsible for a high percentage of airport revenue. Advertising companies pay royalties to place their ads. Parking facilities and duty-free shops generate significant revenue. Without support services, airports wouldn't be commercially viable.

A FRAGMENTED ECOSYSTEM

As we write, aviation support services in Africa are fragmented, involving dozens of small companies with little or no connection to recognized global players. These companies lack international expertise and essential experience. As local organizations, they have no framework of global relationships with airlines or airport operators, meaning that they have no incentive to apply global standards. Worse, they have little leverage with airlines. They often appear interchangeable, making it easy to replace them.

Some of these companies are partly owned by large European companies, but this doesn't mean that they adhere to the same international standards as their parent organizations. They operate independently, with little oversight. Air France-KLM or SN Brussels, for example, might have a management contract with a local player or own a percentage of an African firm, but the operational and line management relationship between the two is very weak.

A lot of these smaller companies appear to have been founded or invested in by European companies with the intention of safeguarding their own interests. If Air France or SN Brussels is flying into an African country, they prefer companies they control to handle and serve their flights and passengers.

Sadly, some of the concessions awarded to these service providers are based on political relationships, with the bidding process handled out of the public eye. These concessions can be quite lucrative. Because they usually don't include clear, binding contracts governing the relationships between concessionaire and government, the concessionaire's obligations and long-term interests are unclear. This breeds a reluctance to invest. Even those who want to invest are stymied by a lack of investment criteria. This results in poor quality of service and a poor safety record.

As an example of the fragmented African market, consider Kinshasa N'djili Airport, which serves fewer than eight hundred thousand passengers per year. While passenger and revenue growth have been stagnant for a decade, the airport supports a total of four ground handling companies. Khartoum, Sudan, serves fewer than two million passengers per year, yet five ground handling companies operate at the airport. To put these numbers in context, compare them with Cairo, which serves more than seventeen million passengers per year using only two ground handling companies. Similarly, more than 8.5 million passengers pass through Casablanca per year, served by only three ground handling companies.

In Kinshasa and Khartoum, fragmentation, combined with a lack of effective regulation, has created a surplus of service providers. The competition is so fierce that none of the individual companies make a reasonable profit margin, so they can't afford to invest in further training or better equipment.

Airlines are the most visible aspect of the aviation ecosystem. As a result, in an effort to please passengers, who are also constituents, most government policy is focused solely on airlines. Very few passengers understand the different elements of an airport's success or are willing to push for improved services.

Despite these limitations, there are a few examples of service companies delivering high quality against the odds. Airline Services and Logistics (ASL), for example, is a catering company that was founded in 1996. In 2012, the company entered into a joint venture with RwandAir, 70 percent owned by the former and 30 percent owned by the latter. In 2014, the company was awarded a fifteen-year concession to provide exclusive catering services to airlines flying in and out of Kigali International Airport. This kind of monopoly might look like a disaster waiting to happen. ASL, however, is a global company, meaning that ASL Nigeria benefits from the expertise and standards of the parent company. This enables them to provide quality service.

Establishing partnerships can break monopolies and lead to better outcomes for everyone involved. Nairobi Airport Services is a joint venture with Servair, one of the global leaders in catering. Despite this, the company is locally owned and not bound by European standards. For many years, Nairobi Airport Services enjoyed a monopoly in Nairobi, providing eleven thousand in-flight meals a day at a cost of between US$6 and US$10 per meal. In 2014, however, the Kenya Airports Authority signed an agreement with a new catering company, LSG Sky Chefs, which is the in-flight catering company of Lufthansa.

The change resulted in a reduction in prices, higher quality services, and increased government revenues.

While these examples illustrate the possibility of change for the better, there are still too many examples of African aviation moving in the opposite direction. Menzies, one of the largest ground handling companies in the world, has a management agreement with AHS, a Senegalese ground handling company with a presence in several West African countries. When the previous Senegalese president lost the recent election, however, controversy swirled around the circumstances in which AHS was awarded the original contract. As a result, AHS and Menzies entered into a legal dispute and the relationship began to decline.

Another growing aspect of the support services industry is cargo handling. According to a report by IATA, issued in March 2017, global demand for freight grew at a rate of 6.9 percent in January 2017, as compared with the same month the previous year. Demand in Africa, however, grew by 24.3 percent year on year in January and 33.7 percent in July 2017, making it the world's fastest growing region. This increase was driven in large part by growth in demand—57 percent year on year—between Africa and Asia.

Growth in available freight tonne kilometers (AFTK) grew by 6.1 percent in Africa over the same period, well above the world average of 3.5 percent. While these statistics are cause for joy, it is important to note that African air cargo still accounts for only 1.6 percent of the world's total. Many factors inhibit the growth in African air cargo, including outdated customs regimes, runways that cannot accommodate larger cargo aircraft, corruption and poor governance, availability of X-ray and other security machines, high production costs, and poor air cargo infrastructure.

The most effective and efficient air cargo facilities are built with both airside and landside access, meaning they are located at the perimeter of the airport. This makes it easy to deliver goods by truck, which are then passed through security and easily stored prior to loading. These facilities should also be able to accommodate perishables—cold storage, freezers, live animals, valuables—specialized large safe boxes, radioactive material, and even an explosives room to store flammable and otherwise dangerous materials.

Few passengers see these facilities, but they exist at all major airports. Airports may have one or more service providers who build and manage the warehouses for air cargo. In Kenya, for example, there are several service providers, including Swissport and Kenya Airways, who recently inaugurated a new cargo facility. Agility, one of the world's leading integrated logistics solutions providers, with more than US$5 billion in revenues, has identified Africa as a strategic imperative, and today employs more than 2,500 people in Africa. It is building warehouses across the continent to support the growth that is taking place, working hand in hand with governments, freight forwarders, airlines, ground handling agents, and other stakeholders.

HOW CAN AFRICA IMPROVE SUPPORT SERVICES?

According to IATA, investing in airlines is a relatively poor bet. On average, they deliver a 4 percent return on capital. Airport support services may be less glamorous than airlines, but they reliably provide a double-digit return on investment of between 10 and 40 percent. Yet, there's a huge gap in the market for midsized companies willing to guarantee quality service. Small, local players can't benefit from economies of scale, lack leverage with airlines, and lose out to global players and even private sector players in terms of efficiency.

At its core, aviation is about provision of experience. It's an exciting sector, based on taking people to new places and opening new opportunities. Without quality support services, it's impossible for airlines to create a positive experience. Economically, this isn't a trivial point. People are willing to pay for good experiences, and the amount of money they will happily part with increases as the quality of those experiences improves. Through high-quality support services, an aviation hub can really distinguish itself and generate economic value.

Support services also create jobs, which can transform airports into growth magnets and create a foundation for economic development. The opportunity exists for investors to generate lucrative returns, while supporting projects that will have indirect impacts on entire countries. What is the best way to encourage investment?

The most important factor is the encouragement of private capital. Private capital brings commercial criteria, which means that companies start to seek out greater efficiency, higher revenue, and better quality of service. This process requires financial discipline and eliminates corruption.

If not handled correctly, however, privatization can go badly. A critical point of the privatization process is the selection of the right private operator. This is illustrated by Bi-Courtney Terminal in Lagos. Bi-Courtney Terminal, also known as Terminal Two or MMA2, is the only terminal at Lagos International Airport that isn't run by the Federal Airports Authority of Nigeria (FAAN). Indeed, with the exception of Warri, it's the only privately run terminal in Nigeria. Following a fire that destroyed the previous domestic terminal at Lagos International Airport, the concession for Terminal Two was put out for bids. The preferred bidder was a Canadian firm named Royal Standerton. But somehow, the concession was eventually awarded to Bi-Courtney, a Nigerian company.

This catalyzed a legal battle between Royal Standerton and the FAAN. Simultaneously, Bi-Courtney entered into a separate legal battle with the FAAN over the duration of the concession. Bi-Courtney claimed it was a thirty-six-year concession, while the FAAN claimed that it was for twelve years. In the end, Bi-Courtney got the terminal, but they also developed a poor relationship with the FAAN. Bi-Courtney claimed that the FAAN should hand over ownership of the state-of-the-art, newly constructed general aviation terminal, as well as damages—amounting to 132 billion Nigerian naira—for unrelated reasons. This situation has inhibited the growth of the Bi-Courtney terminal.

Abidjan International Airport has a much more successful history. In 1996, management and operation of the terminal in Côte d'Ivoire was privatized and awarded to a French company named Aeria. Ownership of Aeria is shared by private investors (65 percent), a technical partner (25 percent), and the state of Côte d'Ivoire (10 percent). The company has invested in infrastructure and delivered quality service, impressing the government so much that the concession has been extended.

Privatizing services may be the most effective way of delivering excellent airport support services, but ultimately what matters more is putting professionals in charge—people who understand the industry, know how to compete, and are equipped to manage concessions effectively.

To control the number of service providers and limit fragmentation, it's a good idea to enact service-level agreements (SLAs) with a limited number of players. When there are too many service providers, each one sees a drop in profits. This, in turn, discourages them from investing in equipment and training, reducing the quality of service to airlines and passengers. The number of players should be commensurate with passenger numbers, neither so many that they are all fighting for scraps or so few that one develops an unhealthy monopoly. Nairobi, for example, has found a good balance by contracting two catering companies to serve the eight million passengers who pass through Nairobi International Airport each year.

Putting SLAs in place also ensures a minimum level of service, along with clarity about how financial returns are shared with the government or airport operator. Governments may choose to ask for up-front payments upon awarding concessions. This strategy enables them to commercialize concessions immediately and invest the funds in aviation-related infrastructure. It's a win-win: a professional, modern airport attracts more passengers, increasing the profits of concessionaires.

Another aspect of successful SLAs is linking royalties with revenue, based on audited financial statements. Some of the best contracts include a clause whereby, every five years, the concessionaire and government must sit down and discuss how well the investor is doing. If, for example, passenger numbers drop drastically due to some macrofactor that negatively affects the concessionaire, the contract can be renegotiated to adjust for the unexpected downturn. This option gives investors comfort and can make them more willing to commit.

Another valuable clause in SLAs is an option to extend concessions. Imagine a ten-year contract. By year eight, the concessionaire will probably become reluctant to invest, due to the uncertainty inherent in a fixed-term contract. They don't know whether their concession will continue long enough for them to reap the benefits of their investment. If their SLA includes an option to extend, they will probably want to impress the government and earn the extension.

Contrary to popular belief, corruption is not rampant in every part of Africa. Many businesses achieve success and make a huge impact without paying bribes. Nonetheless, corruption is undoubtedly a challenge in the African aviation ecosystem. Crafting SLAs can play a significant role in reducing the potential for corruption, as can the creation of operating committees who sit with concessionaires, airport operators, and airlines to discuss problems and find ways to resolve them together.

Almost every emerging market has realized that maintaining open communication, integrity, and close working relationships is very important. Ultimately, the success of concessions relies on the formation and maintenance of quality relationships between service providers and governments or airport operators. For relationships to improve, it's essential that support service providers operate with integrity and leaders understand how support service operators create value. This frame helps everyone in the relationship to see other parties as genuine partners.

Support services have the potential to be the unsung heroes of the African aviation sector. Airlines have a history of government ownership, and therefore a background in which competition was a minor factor. Privatization has led to increasing competition, squeezing profits.

Fuel, one of the biggest costs faced by airlines, is subject to price shocks. In 2014, oil was US$110 per barrel. As we write this book, it's at $40. In the future, it might drop to $10 or go back up to $80 or $100. Additionally, Airbus and Boeing have a virtual monopoly on the manufacture of commercial aircraft, giving them a very strong hand at the negotiating table.

All these factors make running a profitable airline very challenging, a situation exacerbated by the fact that even the most professionally managed airline is prone to macroshocks such as 9/11, bird flu, or Ebola, which can dramatically affect passenger numbers with little warning.

Support services live and die by a different equation. In most of Africa—unlike in Europe, North America, or Asia—they operate on a concession basis. This means that they must compete constantly for concessions; but once they've secured a concession, they are highly motivated to maximize profits.

With a fairer, more transparent approach to allotting concessions, the growth of professional support service companies, and the development of genuine partnerships between airport operators and support service companies, the fragmentation of the industry can be resolved. We envisage an Africa in which appropriately sized support service companies compete to operate the most effective businesses, not for political favors, winning their concessions through quality and earning solid profits, while simultaneously paying a share of revenue to airport operators, who redirect these profits into the development of infrastructure. This will create a virtuous circle in which support services companies provide dignified, well-paid jobs and African aviation becomes safer and more pleasurable.

PACKAGING AVIATION IN AFRICA FOR CITIZENS AND BUSINESSES

With the exception of Antarctica, Africa is the most poorly served continent on the planet in terms of aviation. It has the least-developed infrastructure and the highest ticket prices. This doesn't necessarily mean, however, that it offers low investment potential.

Conventional wisdom suggests that the most valuable investments are to be found in developed markets. These markets, however, are often so saturated that it's hard to find untapped opportunities. The real potential lies in so-called blue oceans, new markets with enormous development capacity. The difficulty is that these opportunities can be hard to identify.

An India author named C. K. Prahalad reinforced this point in his book *Fortune at the Bottom of the Pyramid*, in which he challenged the belief that markets in developing countries must look like markets in developed countries. Specifically, international companies often sell products in large packages. These are too large for individual consumers, meaning that the products may not be popular.

Companies used to delivering in bulk may conclude that there is no opportunity in these markets. As Prahalad points out, however, companies can benefit from offering smaller packages. Single servings of oil, sugar, or milk, for example, may entice people to make purchases, while simultaneously yielding a healthy profit margin. In developing countries, local markets are usually built on daily incomes, as opposed to weekly or monthly salaries. People may not have the disposable income to invest in large packages, but that doesn't mean they lack interest in the products.

How does this apply to aviation? In Africa, the market doesn't always operate along the smooth lines common in Europe and other developed regions. Companies wishing to deliver services must align with the realities of the local market. Many Africans use only cash to pay for goods. A travel agency that insists they must purchase tickets using a credit card will miss the opportunity to reach thousands of potential customers.

Satguru Travel, a company that we will discuss in greater detail later in the book, illustrates this scenario. The company has become very successful because it understands African customers very well. Tickets may be paid for using cash, and Satguru provides packages to alleviate the stresses and challenges many Africans experience when they contemplate travel. The company provides visa services, for example, facilitating a transaction that usually involves layers of bureaucracy and may confuse the average traveler. Satguru also books hotels for layovers in Dubai and provides many other services African travelers normally can't purchase using cash.

This is a win-win. Through adapting to the African market, Satguru enables many people who wouldn't ordinarily be able to travel to do so. The company benefits by earning a significant profit on transactions, aided by the fact that it has little competition. With so many people in Africa still without credit cards, or not yet comfortable sharing credit card information online, Satguru has stolen a march on competitors by catering to the consumer.

The reverse of this scenario is seen in numerous African airport lounges. Despite the fact that many travelers without credit cards would gladly pay fifty or a hundred dollars to access lounges, many don't allow cash transactions. If African airport services are to grow, the industry as a whole must understand its customers and meet them where they are.

POOR CONNECTIVITY LIMITS AVIATION GROWTH

African aviation is hindered by a lack of connectivity. The average African airport serves far fewer cities than a similar-sized airport in Europe, North America, or Asia. As described earlier, this presents real problems for travelers. Another recent business trip Hassan intended to undertake involved travel from Dar es Salaam in Tanzania to Kinshasa in the DRC. A direct flight between the two cities would take perhaps four hours, but there is no direct flight. Instead, Hassan was forced to book tickets from Dar es Salaam to Istanbul, Turkey, then another seven-hour flight from Istanbul to Kinshasa. The poor connectivity of African cities increased his journey time by more than ten hours, causing inconvenience, fatigue, and a loss of time that he could have spent productively or with his family.

Some of the reasons for the lack of connectivity can be found in the size of African cities. Most are both smaller and poorer than Asian and European cities, with only six home to more than ten million inhabitants. Even in those larger cities, two-thirds of the population live in slums. Air travel appears to them as an impossible dream. With fifty-four African countries, each with their own capital cities, the populace is spread across the diaspora. This means that there are few hubs—perhaps ten—with the size and economic capacity to justify a high level of air connectivity.

There are signs that this is beginning to change, however. As Africa becomes both more urbanized and more global, the demand for air connectivity will surely increase. The African middle class has the potential to become the largest in the world. More than one in three Africans have entered the middle class in the past decade, and thanks to rapid economic growth, their numbers are set to swell further. At least 370 million Africans, or 34 percent of the continent's 1.1 billion people, are now middle class. This emergent class will help drive further economic growth and development: by 2060, the group should represent 42 percent of the population.

As these people become more affluent, they will certainly wish to travel, at which point it will become apparent how much value air travel offers the continent. Much of Africa consists of difficult terrain, making it almost impossible to traverse by land. In addition, one-third of African countries are landlocked. For them, maritime travel isn't an option. Air travel solves both of these problems at a stroke.

One positive example is the signature of a memorandum of understanding between Uganda, Rwanda, and South Sudan in 2014. Under the terms of the agreement, which was signed in Kampala, Uganda, pending a final binding agreement, airlines will be allowed fifth freedom rights between the airports of the respective countries. Fifth freedom allows airlines from each country to transport passengers between the other two countries. The three countries listed above signed a further agreement with Kenya shortly thereafter, which was successfully translated into a final agreement—with Kenya a signatory—in December 2015. Since then, the number of flights between Rwanda and Uganda has increased at least threefold.

MEETING THE GROWING DEMAND FOR AFRICAN AVIATION

If businesses are to meet demand for aviation in Africa as it develops, they must package their services to meet the needs of potential customers. Ticket prices, for example, must be adjusted to reflect the incomes of Africans. If it costs a thousand dollars to travel a thousand miles across Europe, it can't also cost a thousand dollars to travel a thousand miles across Africa. Africa's average GDP is far lower than Europe's, so it's not realistic for airline tickets to be priced similarly. This is a huge opportunity for low-cost airlines. The current penetration of low-cost carriers in Africa is far lower than any other continent in the world. With a little foresight and the desire to serve a burgeoning middle class, huge opportunities exist at the bottom of the pyramid.

While African aviation infrastructure is moving in the right direction, there is still a considerable gulf between the level of aviation services offered on the continent in 2017 and the level they need to reach if more African people are to become regular travelers. While infrastructure is essential to a viable aviation sector, professional services are just as important and often overlooked. Infrastructure is Africa's ticket to the global aviation game, but without improved services the continent will be a perennial loser. Quality services will play an essential role in winning the game.

CHAPTER SEVEN

THE CHANGING FACE OF AFRICA'S TOP CARRIERS

The history of African aviation makes it clear that there are numerous pitfalls for prospective carriers. Perhaps no airline illustrates this more profoundly than Air Afrique. In 2001, the *Economist* ran an article stating that "Everyone who works in Africa has a horror story about flying with Air Afrique." For Eric, this could hardly be more apt.

In 1997, Eric planned a trip home from Canada to Côte d'Ivoire at Christmas. He flew with Air Afrique, previously one of the continent's most well-respected airlines. At the time, Eric happened to be at school with the son of one of the airline's commercial directors. This young man convinced a group of people, including some friends who were getting married, to fly with Air Afrique. Unfortunately, the experience was a disaster.

The connecting flight from Canada to New York passed smoothly. Once the flight landed at JFK, however, troubles quickly escalated. Unsuspecting passengers were told that there were mechanical problems, although they later discovered that the problem was far more straightforward. Air Afrique had overbooked during peak season and lacked the capacity to transport all their customers in a timely fashion. Tempers quickly frayed, and the situation turned into the biggest mess Eric had ever witnessed at JFK, with frustrated passengers shouting and fighting.

Finally, after eighteen hours, Eric boarded his flight. He was seated by the window in the very last row, next to the lavatories. The seat itself was in poor condition, and the entire airplane interior was poorly maintained. Arriving in Dakar, he hoped the nightmare was over. In fact, it was just beginning.

Most of the passengers from the flight between New York and Dakar were continuing to Abidjan, but the aircraft on which they were booked was only about a third of the size of the one they had just deplaned. There was a huge backlog of luggage from several earlier flights, so the only luggage that could be loaded on to the airplane belonged to the crew and to people who had already left Dakar and had been waiting two or three days for their luggage to catch up with them.

When the plane finally landed in Abidjan, passengers were understandably furious. As they waited for their luggage to emerge, a crew member recognized the son of the commercial director, so he came over and told Eric and the commercial director's son, "Don't bother waiting for your luggage. It won't arrive today. We'll figure out a way to get it to you, maybe tomorrow or the day after." The bride of the wedding party burst into tears. Her wedding dress didn't arrive until after the wedding.

This whole situation looks particularly unfortunate when contrasted with Eric's experience a scant four years earlier. As an undergrad, he took the same journey home from Canada to Côte d'Ivoire. At that time, the company was beginning to exhibit problems, but it was functional. On his second trip, Eric was shocked by the degree to which it had deteriorated in such a short space of time.

This cautionary tale demonstrates the importance of consistent governance and management. Air Afrique was founded as a Pan-African airline, with the intention of demonstrating the continent's emerging confidence and capability. Yet, five years after Eric's disastrous Christmas flight, it was in liquidation. All five thousand employees lost their jobs.

In many ways, the history of Air Afrique is synonymous with the history of air transport in Africa. Conceived in 1960, it was a joint venture between Air France, Union Aéromaritime de Transport, and eleven West and Central African countries, under the auspices of the Ivorian president Félix Houphouët-Boigny. At its peak in the 1970s and '80s, Air Afrique employed more than five thousand people, operated more than fifteen aircraft, and served close to a million passengers annually. The airline flew to twenty-two African destinations and nine international destinations, including New York, Geneva, London, Paris, and Rome.

Until the mid-1990s, Air Afrique was considered one of the most reputable African carriers. Its steady decline, however, visible from the early 1980s, accelerated in the 1990s. By 2002, it was officially declared bankrupt, with debts totaling US$500 million. Despite influential macroshocks, such as the global slowdown of the airline industry following 9/11, industry analysts agree that the company's downfall resulted primarily from mismanagement. One of Air Afrique's greatest failings was overemployment.

Compare Air Afrique's fifteen aircraft and five thousand employees with Kenya Airways. In 2017, the latter operates more than forty aircraft and employs only four thousand employees. Air Afrique's overstaffing arose because the airline was owned by eleven different countries, and company leaders wanted to hire people from their own countries. If the company hired an Ivorian pilot, Senegalese leaders would push for the employment of a Senegalese pilot. The same dynamic would repeat, with other countries pushing for representations.

The president of Senegal, Abdoulaye Wade, said in 1996 that Air Afrique was a toy of the post-independence era. Indeed, West Africans were proud of Air Afrique's success. The existence of a Pan-African airline catered to the egos of citizens and leaders.

All of which makes it even sadder that Air Afrique collapsed in such ignominy. The airline's final CEO was Jeffrey Erickson, an American-born aviation expert who spoke no French and had never worked in Africa. During his final days, he announced massive layoffs. In retaliation, his own staff barred him from boarding Air Afrique flights. To leave Africa, he was forced to drive from Ghana to Abidjan and travel on a different airline.

AN INDUSTRY IN FLUX: SUCCESSES, CHALLENGES, AND POSSIBILITIES

The African aviation industry continues to be unpredictable. Previously strong airlines are struggling, while others are rising to take their place. At the time of writing, it's hard to know exactly where EgyptAir fits into this framework.

The company was the first African airline and the seventh airline in the world. Today, it is a state-owned company, although special legislation permits it to operate independently of government bureaucracy and ensures that it is self-financing. The government also established the Ministry of Civil Aviation, with the intention of modernizing its aviation infrastructure.

At the behest of the Egyptian government, which realized the importance of aviation to the nation's tourism industry and overall economic development, EgyptAir was transformed into a holding company, with its own board and a clear governance structure. This holding company has played a key role in the success of EgyptAir. The company also has subsidiaries in several sectors, including maintenance and engineering, ground services, flight services, tourism, duty-free, and medical services. Supplementary industries operate EgyptAir's fleet of more than sixty aircraft, which serve eighty destinations, nineteen of which are in Egypt.

Unfortunately, 2016 saw Egypt experience three alarming aviation incidents. The first occurred in March 2016, when a domestic EgyptAir flight was hijacked and forced to divert to Cyprus. In May of the same year, a flight between Cairo and Paris crashed into the Mediterranean, killing everyone on board. Finally, a Russian charter jet crashed shortly after takeoff from Sharm El Sheikh. In addition, the political situation in Egypt has placed pressure on the aviation industry. Nonetheless, EgyptAir and the Egyptian aviation sector have so far proven resilient. It remains to be seen whether they will ride out the issues they are currently facing and emerge stronger.

South African Airways is in a similar situation. One of the continent's flagship airlines, it has recently faced serious challenges. The company was established in 1934 after the government's acquisition of Union Airways. Union's founder and former CEO, Major Allister Miller, was a World War I flying ace who was forced to sell the company after one of its aircraft crashed, killing almost everyone on board.

From its inception, South African Airways grew steadily, serving destinations as distant as Australia and Hong Kong. During the apartheid era, however, the airline faced hostility around the world. In the United States, the comprehensive Anti-Apartheid Act of 1986 forbade the airline from landing in the United States. Australia soon followed suit, forcing South African Airways to suspend services to Perth and Sydney. The company's offices in London were also attacked during this period.

When apartheid ended, South African Airways entered a new era. It resumed its former network of flights and was named the Best Airline to Africa by London's *Executive Traveller* magazine in 1991. The company's golden age came between 2004 and 2006. During this period, it applied for membership of the Star Alliance and, after meeting fifty-four individual criteria, was accepted. This made it the first African airline to gain membership of the alliance—EgyptAir and Ethiopian Airlines have since followed suit. South African Airways was also the first non-Saudi airline to fly directly into Medina in Saudi Arabia for the busy Hajj season.

Unfortunately, this period was followed by a series of restructuring efforts, prompted by poor financial performance. Between 2006 and 2013, the airline underwent ten different restructuring plans and employed a total of eight CEOs, several of whom ended their tenures ignominiously. Unprofitable routes, such as Johannesburg-Dakar-Washington, DC-Dallas, were discontinued, while profitable routes, such as Johannesburg-Accra-Washington, DC, were expanded.

A June 2016 report, by the Centre for Aviation, highlighted government meddling as a common problem preventing airlines from making strong commercial and strategic decisions.[11] The report specifically mentioned South African Airways as a company adversely affected by government interference. The most recent recovery plan was founded on a new partnership with Emirates, which would have given South African Airways a much stronger network and a guaranteed revenue stream. Despite months of negotiations, South African Airways' chairwoman failed to appear at the agreement's signing ceremony

---

11 "Africa Outlook," Centre for Aviation, accessed October 13, 2017, https://centreforaviation.com/insights/analysis/africa-outlook-ethiopian-airlines-and-air-mauritius-grow-but-others-face-strong-headwinds-282282

in Paris, causing the deal to fall through. According to media reports, this turn of events cost South African Airways approximately US$164 million.

As of 2017, Emirates' seat capacity into South Africa was greater than the capacity of the entire South African Airways long-haul network. Between June 6 and June 12, 2016, Emirates flew aircraft with a total of 36,456 seats into South Africa, whereas South African Airways' total seat capacity was 30,704. Although overall losses in 2016 were reduced in comparison with previous years, the struggling South African economy and fluctuations in oil prices represent further struggles for South African Airways.

It's not all bad news for Africa's most well-established carriers, however. Ethiopian Airlines was founded in 1945 as a wholly owned company of the government of Ethiopia. The company was the brainchild of Emperor Haile Selassie, who wanted to create a national carrier to show the world that an African nation was capable of running a successful airline and as an antidote to perceptions of the continent as poverty-stricken. Originally, Ethiopian was managed by Trans World Airlines (TWA) but has been independent since 1970, when TWA stepped back into the role of adviser.

Today, the airline continues to expand. In 2012, Ethiopian became the major shareholder of ASKY, an airline based in Lomé, Togo. Three years later, the company obtained a management agreement to run ASKY. In 2013, Ethiopian acquired a 49 percent stake in the new Malawian Airlines. On top of this, Ethiopian has diversified its operations into aircraft maintenance, pilot training, ground handling, and more. The company joined the Star Alliance in 2011, and in 2012, the *Economist* published an article titled, "Ethiopian Dares to Dream."[12] The article concluded with the words, "It could be the example that others follow. Ethiopian has not just Africa but the whole world in its hands."

The airline serves more African destinations than any other carrier, with nineteen domestic routes, eighty-two passenger destinations, and twenty-three freighter destinations. In terms of fleet size, Ethiopian is Africa's largest airline, beating out Kenya Airways and South African Airways. The company offers the world's second longest route, Addis Ababa to Toronto, along with the second shortest, Malabo to Douala, and served as Africa's launch customer for the Boeing 787. The company acquired six 787 Dreamliners in a deal funded by EXIM Bank in the United States, valued at US$2 billion.

In 2013 and 2014, Ethiopian was rated the most profitable airline in Africa and the eighteenth most popular in the world. While the African sector overall has accumulated losses of $1.5 billion in the eight years to 2017, Ethiopian has accumulated profits of

---

[12] Gulliver, "Ethiopian Dares to Dream," *The Economist*, September 3, 2012, https://www.economist.com/blogs/gulliver/2012/09/ethiopian-airlines

$800 million. This success has been achieved with consistency, commitment, and foresight. By October 2006, for example, the company had concluded a total of eighty-four bilateral service agreements, thirteen of them with European countries and the rest with African countries.

The company's success can be partly attributed to the fact that throughout its seventy years, the Ethiopian government has resisted the temptation to interfere in the management of the airline, and it has never succumbed to undue political influence. Even the Marxist Derg—the coordinating committee of the armed forces, police, and territorial army that ruled Ethiopia between 1974 and 1987—allowed the airline to run on a strictly commercial basis. In 1988, the *Christian Science Monitor* described the airline as a "capitalist success in Marxist Ethiopia." Even in 1991, the year in which the Communist government was violently overthrown, the airline still succeeded in posting a profit.

If Ethiopia stands as an example of African aviation at its finest, the lack of low-cost carriers is the continent's Achilles' heel. Fastjet aims to address this limitation, although as of 2017, there is still much work to be done before it succeeds.

The history of fastjet begins with an airline named Fly540, the vision of entrepreneur Stelios Haji-Ioannou. Haji-Ioannou founded easyJet and has described Africa as aviation's last frontier. Fly540 was incorporated in 2005 by Don Smith and Nixon Ooko in Nairobi and had its maiden flight in 2006 to Mombasa.

Lonrho PLC, established in Africa in 1909 as the London and Rhodesian Mining Company, subsequently acquired 49 percent of Fly540 for a mere US$1.5 million. As the primary shareholders, they established two subsidiaries, Fly540 Ghana and Fly540 Angola. In 2009, however, Lonrho reported a loss of $7.5 million after tax on Fly540. By 2011, that loss grew to $19 million. According to media reports, 60 percent of the 2011 loss came as a result of the new franchises in Ghana and Angola. The company also lost $2 million from the establishment of Fly540 Uganda, which never got off the ground. Literally, no Fly540 Uganda flights ever took off. In June 2016, Lonrho announced the sale of its stake in Fly540 to Rubicon Investments for $85 million.

At that point, Fly540 evolved into fastjet. Armed with ambitious plans, a sizable treasure chest, years of experience, and access both to its existing bases in Kenya, Tanzania, Angola, and Ghana and to hubs in Europe, the company sought to stake a claim to dominion over the last frontier of aviation. Fastjet, however, reckoned without stiff competition from the legacy state-owned carriers and the governments that owned them. For this reason, the company was denied landing rights in some of its main target locations.

In 2015, fastjet's CEO insisted that "Liberalization must come to Africa. We could have increased our network and brought nations reliable value travel, if not for the level of protectionism in Africa." He attacked national carriers, demanding that governments explained why they continued to subsidize loss-making airlines such as Kenya Airways and South African Airways, when the money would be better spent on roads and health care. Why, he asked, did they not leave the private sector to invest in airlines? "Governments can't run airlines," he said. "It's a proven fact. Let private enterprise take its course. You will get a much better aviation landscape, and competition is good for everyone."[13]

In reality, cumbersome government intervention is only part of the reason for fastjet's bumpy ride so far. It's true that resistance from governments has limited the company to eleven cities, only four of which—Dar es Salaam, Nairobi, Johannesburg, and Entebbe—are major airports. Another major factor in its struggles, however, is the company's base. Until 2016, the management and main operations were based at London Gatwick, far from its core market.

Following an announcement that company results were below market expectations, this was to change. Haji-Ioannou sent a letter to the company's chairman, calling for a meeting. Haji-

---

[13] Sibusiso Tshabalala, "African Governments Are Making It Difficult for Low-Cost Airlines to Thrive," *Quartz Africa*, November 3, 2015, https://qz.com/539440/african-governments-are-making-it-difficult-for-low-cost-airlines-to-thrive/

Ioannou claimed that he was losing trust in the company's management, citing an extremely high cost base and expenditure of £80 million in three years. Following Haji-Ioannou's intervention, the company's CEO, Ed Winter, left the company, handing the reins to a South African named Nico Bezuidenhout, the former CEO of the low-cost South African airline Mango. Bezuidenhout laid out plans to bring the company's finances under control, focusing on the distribution network, refining the cost structure, evaluating and matching fees to market demand, and moving the company's head offices back to Africa from Gatwick.

Despite its teething troubles and the infighting to which the company's management has sometimes been prone, fastjet has developed a visible economic presence in at least one African country—Tanzania. In 2013, fastjet served thirty thousand passengers per month. By 2015, that number was closer to sixty-five thousand per month. By the end of 2016, fastjet operated regular flights within Tanzania, and into Kenya, Zambia, Comoros, Malawi, and South Africa. Will fastjet succeed in making a serious impact in the African market? Time will tell.

WHAT FACTORS BRING AFRICAN CARRIERS SUCCESS?

As this chapter draws to a close, let's summarize the overall state of Africa's carriers. Some, like EgyptAir, Kenya Airways, and South African, have experienced considerable success but face an uncertain future. Others, like fastjet, are still striving to establish a successful business model and achieve penetration. Air Côte d'Ivoire, Royal Air Maroc, and RwandAir show real potential, while Ethiopian is a clear standout, withstanding political volatility to experiencing consistent success for more than seventy years.

What can the emerging stars, along with other ambitious airlines, learn from Ethiopian? What commonalities can we identify from the history of Ethiopian, as well as during the successful periods of EgyptAir and South African Airways? We believe that the most important factor is governance. Airlines may be government owned, but they must not operate as extensions of a government. This protects them from the infighting that often characterizes politics and from becoming pawns in the power struggles of politicians. Successful airlines operate as professional, independent, commercially driven enterprises. For African carriers to achieve lasting success, this model must become far more common on the continent.

Ethiopian provides a model to which other African carriers can aspire. By consistently maintaining world-class standards and forging international partnerships, the company has built an exceptionally strong reputation. It has shown both ambition and determination, sustaining those qualities for more than seven decades. EgyptAir and South African Airways have shown that

African airlines can thrive when they are well managed, while fastjet holds the promise of a fresh model. As of 2017, however, the fastjet model is still in its infancy, and EgyptAir and South African Airways have storms to weather. Africa needs more champions willing to take a stand for quality and longevity.

# SECTION FOUR

SOLUTIONS FOR AVIATION IN AFRICA

CHAPTER EIGHT

NURTURING AVIATION CHAMPIONS IN AFRICA

The challenge facing aviation in Africa is one familiar to many sectors, not only across the continent but also around the world. It's the challenge of transforming potential into reality. One of the most powerful approaches, both within Africa and in other industries, regions, and countries, is harnessing the creative power of the private sector. For aviation, this will require the creation of a model that appeals to investors, encouraging them to inject capital into the sector and support it as it grows.

This model will need to go beyond the standard concept of private sector investment. Specifically, we believe that for

Africa's potential to be realized, the aviation sector in Africa needs business champions with clear long-term vision. These champions will need to be spread across multiple segments of the aviation market, from the most visible to the least well known. Can this evolution take place? We believe that it must. This chapter will focus on several examples, both from Africa and other developing regions, to illustrate what's possible.

HOW CHAMPIONS CAN SHAPE BUSINESS ECOSYSTEMS

Business champions provide quality leadership, which is manifested through the presence of a qualified, committed team and a supportive, inclusive culture. Driven by vision, not merely profit, they operate with a clear set of values, such as integrity and honesty. Business champions also stand out due to the quality of their strategic thinking and their capacity to execute based on strategic principles.

Why are business champions such an essential part of the ecosystem? Because they provide examples for others to emulate. As they become world class, their innovations inspire other players in the economy to do things differently, to do things better. You've probably used products made by companies such as Apple, Microsoft, Samsung, and Hyundai. These companies are examples of business champions. Where they lead, others follow. We need similar companies in the African aviation sector, organizations that believe in making the world a better place and have a clear plan of how they wish to do that.

We've already heaped praise on Ethiopian Airlines in previous chapters, and for good reason. The company stands unrivaled in the pantheon of African aviation success stories. Now, let's look more closely at how Ethiopian operates as a champion of the aviation sector.

First, the company has maintained good relationships with employees and labor unions. In 2012, Ethiopian managed to persuade their workforce to accept pay cuts. Compare this with Kenya Airways, which for years has been locked in battle with unions over the dismissal of staff, pay cuts, and other employment issues. Why were the staff of Ethiopian more willing to accept pay cuts? In our view, they feel like part of a large family, so they were willing to take a long-term outlook and make sacrifices to continue being a part of Ethiopian's success story, trusting that they would be rewarded in better times.

Second, Ethiopian has a more balanced route network than major competitors. Although the company serves approximately the same number of destinations as Kenya Airways, only a third of its revenue is derived from Africa. For Kenya Airways, this number is about half. At the same time, Ethiopian benefits from a larger domestic network than Kenya Airways, with fifteen domestic destinations to Kenya's five.

Third, Ethiopian has built strong relationships with other African countries and airlines. The company's 49 percent stake in Malawian Airlines gives them control of Malawian's management. Their investment in ASKY, based out of Lomé, Togo, also gives them a presence in West Africa. Finally, Ethiopian's excellent governance structure, which shields the company from government interference, is a key differentiator.

Even when Ethiopia suffered from drought or famine, the company continued to fly the flag for Ethiopia on the global stage, providing prestige, profit, and belief. Ultimately, the company's seven decades of success is founded on the original vision of Emperor Haile Selassie. He convinced the people of Ethiopia that the airline could become a national success story, of which everyone could feel a part. As a result, it has become a source of national pride for generations of Ethiopians.

The success of business champions feeds the success of the environment in which they operate, creating a ripple effect of greater economic impact. Every successful business must pay taxes and create jobs, of course, but the opportunities created by champions run deeper. To use Ethiopian as an example once again, many small hotels have opened to serve passengers with layovers in Addis Ababa. Every time we've flown into Addis Ababa, we've stayed at a different hotel, all courtesy of Ethiopian Airlines. These hotels owe a lot of their success to the prosperity of the airline.

Even a single champion in a sector creates a multiplier effect. When an airline is successful, the company's employees earn higher salaries. This enables them to travel. Simultaneously, the airline brings in tourists, who will spend money in hotels. This influx of financing allows hotels to invest in better facilities and improved wages. Hotel staff, benefiting from these improved wages, can treat their families to dinner at local restaurants. Every dollar circulates several times in the local economy. This is what we mean by the multiplier effect.

Champions also reveal untapped potential to others. A successful business champion in Tanzania might encourage a successful champion in Rwanda, who may subsequently encourage a successful champion in the DRC. At each step, they will create jobs requiring more skills, while forcing their competitors to up their game. In this way, champions encourage greater professionalism and an overall improvement in the quality of services across the entire industry.

In the same way that a star athlete energizes and inspires their team, business champions alter the chemistry of ecosystems. Africa is the continent with the largest untapped potential and air transport is a key pillar of that potential. A thriving aviation sector could open and connect Africa's markets and facilitate trade, enabling firms to increase productivity and connect with global supply chains. Air transport can play an important role in everything that Africa wants to achieve, from boosting tourism to exporting agricultural goods. A few business champions could alter the atmosphere of Africa's entire aviation sector.

Most non-African countries have overlooked this potential, focusing on more established markets, where they feel more comfortable. Hassan's company, National Aviation Services (NAS), recognizes and seeks to change this dynamic. Sometimes NAS accepts projects that are not immediately profitable because the company's management believe in tapping into Africa's growth potential and because they value broadening the company's portfolio.

One of NAS's landmark investments, for example, came in Abidjan as Côte d'Ivoire was emerging from years of conflict. For the country as a whole, this was an important development. The government proved that it could run a transparent and open bidding process. When NAS chose to submit a proposal, the potential for development in Côte d'Ivoire was further confirmed. Ultimately, NAS invested US$35 million, split between royalties to the government, new equipment, and financing for infrastructure.

People who use the airport have noticed a significant difference. They've seen the new buses and new equipment and experienced the new VIP service where staff welcome travelers as they get out of their cars. They've been whisked through the departure terminal, a process that simplifies the complicated steps most travelers pass through at the airport.

In the process of transforming Abidjan's airport, NAS took over an existing company, retraining the existing staff and giving them new uniforms, and sent some of the managers to Kuwait for higher-level training. When a new player arrives in an ecosystem and promotes higher standards in this way, they show other players how good things can truly be.

NAS has played an important role in the development of the airport in Abidjan, but it's not the only company that has made a difference. The government of Côte d'Ivoire has privatized management of the airport, contracting it to Aeria. This is despite the fact that Air Côte d'Ivoire's financial position remains somewhat precarious. In terms of service quality, passenger experience, and on-time performance, Aeria is doing an excellent job.

Since the 2011 post-election crisis, the economy of Côte d'Ivoire has been improving, which naturally plays an important role in the development of the aviation sector. One key milestone was the 2014 relocation of the African Development Bank from Tunis to Abidjan. This may not initially appear to be a major accomplishment, but it's a perfect example of the multiplier effect. Consider the number of business travelers who need to attend meetings at the African Development Bank, the amount of travel undertaken by each employee of the bank, and Abidjan's attractiveness as a conference venue, due to the bank's presence. Relocating just one major bank has created a huge influx of passengers into Abidjan's airport.

Satguru Travel, discussed in chapter six, serves as another example of a business champion. Satguru was founded in Kigali in 1989. Today, the company is established in fifty countries worldwide, has an annual turnover of US$600 million, and employs sixteen thousand people. While the company has created a network of agencies across the continent where individuals can purchase tickets, it also serves institutions, including UN offices, the African Development Bank, and other businesses and institutions.

Satguru's success is built on outstanding customer service. Customers can call them in the middle of the night and receive a response to their queries. As we've discussed, the company allows travelers to pay using cash and happily prebooks services that their customers might otherwise find difficult to access, such as tours and safaris. Compounding these advantages, Satguru is led by a young, dynamic team with a finger on the pulse of African travel. The company actively seeks out talented, dedicated individuals and promotes them.

Eric first encountered the company in 2002 in Kigali. At the time, one of the company's travel agents particularly impressed Eric. The man's responsibilities were limited, but he excelled at every task he undertook. To this point, he has ascended to become the head of Satguru's entire East African operations, traveling frequently to the United States. His success, and Satguru's, is built on a foundation of meritocracy. Many people who worked as travel agents in the company's early years have grown into strong, competent managers, some of whom have opened offices in the United States.

The company refuses to rest on its laurels, however, continuing to improve its systems. Billing, for example, used to be somewhat disorganized. This made it difficult for customers to know how much they owed and easily settle bills. As of 2017, Satguru sends out monthly statements to customers, a step on the road toward becoming a fully integrated, full-service travel agency.

This kind of success is made possible by the company's vision, a vision that has taken it even into countries where nobody else wants to do business, such as Sierra Leone. Travelers know that no matter where in Africa they find themselves, the chances are that they'll be able to find a branch of Satguru.

WHAT ARE THE COMMON STRENGTHS OF BUSINESS CHAMPIONS?

There are several ways in which Ethiopian, NAS, and Satguru are similar. All three companies are led by people who look beyond statistics and headlines, making strategic choices for the good of their own companies and for the continent as a whole. These leaders believe that Africa is a place where they can marry profit and purpose, so they choose to make investments that will lead them to success in the long term. They constantly look for ways in which they can improve, promoting best practices and high standards while customizing their services to the African context.

These business leaders take care to forge productive relationships, including with governments. Hassan has invested a lot of time meeting with leaders, and he's constantly in search of ideas to improve countries' performance. This is true even in sectors that are unrelated to the core business of NAS. Ethiopian Airlines has succeeded in maintaining good relationships with successive Ethiopian governments, even the Communists. Some of Satguru's biggest clients, meanwhile, are governments. This presents an obvious challenge. What leverage does Satguru have if government clients fail to pay invoices? Very little. Yet, the company continues to develop mutually beneficial relationships.

As emerging champions in the aviation sector consider their strategies, they must learn from these insights and examples. Traditional business wisdom will not be enough to uplift the aviation sector in Africa. They will need to truly embrace the realities and challenges of the continent and genuinely wish to make the continent a better place.

Too many businesses with an interest in Africa approach the continent with a colonialist mentality. They view Africa as a corrupt, war-ridden, famine-stricken part of the world and treat an enormous, diverse continent as though it were a single small country. It's not. It consists of fifty-four different countries, each with their own past, present, and future. Not every part of Africa is poverty-stricken, war-torn, or corrupt. The continent is home to a great deal of positive energy and many opportunities.

Companies that assume they can do business in Africa in the same way they would in Europe are in for a shock. They must come to Africa with a willingness to learn about what the continent needs and what is already working. When locals feel that they are understood, they will also be willing to learn about approaches that are working in other places, but European and American companies must resist the temptation to assume that they know best. There must be learning on both sides.

When NAS started working in Abidjan, the company took sixteen local trainers to Kuwait to teach them best practices. A few weeks later, NAS's training director in Kuwait commented, "We're learning as much from them as they are learning from us." That's a sustainable mentality. Companies cannot arrive with a ten thousand-page manual and say, "This is how things are going to happen moving forward." They need to learn about the local environment, the local culture, and local best practices, so they can adapt their own best practices, policies, procedures, and systems to the country or city they want to operate in.

Companies with the ambition of influencing the aviation ecosystem for years to come also need to develop a pipeline of leaders from the continent. Diversity is important, so bringing in some leaders from outside of Africa is valuable. Equally important are gender and age diversity. A common mistake, however, is for companies to arrive in Africa and appoint their entire senior leadership teams from their home countries. While they usually hire local staff, the GM, the CEO, the CFO, and the head of HR all come from outside Africa. Over the long haul, this will leave African aviation reliant on talent from abroad. True diversity means finding the best person for every job, wherever that person comes from.

Another essential part of success in Africa is flexibility. NAS has the advantage of hailing from the Middle East, another emerging market, so many of the company's leaders intuitively understand this requirement. Too many companies wishing to invest in Africa fail to recognize the necessity of flexibility. They take the attitude that the contract is law and anything outside of it is non-negotiable. As a result, they burn bridges and fail to build the relationships they need to thrive. Africa has a bright future, but it is still developing. At times, special scenarios and unusual requests will emerge. Companies that are unwilling to address these scenarios will experience difficulties.

WHY HAS AFRICA STRUGGLED AND HOW CAN IT CHANGE?

It would be too optimistic to imagine that African business champions will find life easy. There are reasons why the continent has struggled to produce champions until now. Let's address those reasons.

Consider the case of Fly Blue Crane. The founder of that company, Siza Mzimela, was the first black woman to own an airline. Her goal, in her own words, was to connect "the increasingly commercially significant provincial and regional capitals of South Africa."[14] To achieve this goal, she founded the airline with the intention of offering a consistent, reliable low-cost option. The company started with two 50-foot ERJ 145 aircraft operating out of Johannesburg and flying directly to Kimberly, Bloemfontein, Nelspruit, and other domestic destinations. Fly Blue Crane launched in 2015 with the slogan, "A fresh approach." The company operated for approximately a year and a half but, in March 2017, grounded their aircraft to restructure the company. As of August 2017, Fly Blue Crane remains grounded and hasn't provided a time line for restarting operations.

At first glance, it seems the company did a lot of things right. It presented a fresh, appealing image, offered popular routes at

---

14 Renee Ash, "Siza Mzimela: First Black Woman CEO of a Commercial Airline," Black Pages, December 2, 2015, https://www.blackpages.co.za/news/item/73-siza-mzimela-first-black-woman-ceo-of-a-commercial-airline

good prices, and ran catchy ad slogans, such as, "Our Joburg-Cape Town direct flights are filling up fast! If you're dreaming of a beach holiday, you'd better start clicking."

Yet, something clearly wasn't working. Why did Fly Blue Crane cease operations, and why hasn't the company started flying again? Several factors seem to have contributed to the situation. South Africa's economy has been faring poorly, with the rand depreciating in value. The country is mired in political infighting. Additionally, there is intense competition from South African Airways and the company's low-cost subsidiary, Mango.

As Africa struggles to develop business champions, many people see a lack of government support as the root of their challenges. To an extent, this is undoubtedly the case. There is a general perception that aviation is for Western companies or for government-backed enterprises. As a result, many would-be champions believe that the lack of political will to support the private sector is crucial. They lament low access to capital, poor fiscal incentives, and limited access to markets.

Admittedly, these incentives would make it easier for private investors to launch into business, but they might also distort motivation. Most of the companies that have benefited from preferential government support have, like Air Afrique, faded and died. Almost every African airport is home to at least one significant, connected player that has received some form of concession. Yet, these concessions rapidly change hands, placing the recipients in an insecure position.

Aviation is a highly regulated sector, and no company, no matter how visionary, can succeed if they are in direct competition with the government, or if they're engaged in multiple energy-sapping battles before they even begin to do business. Governments in Africa must update their understanding of what is required for aviation to thrive, and this will only happen when they fully understand that aviation can transform entire economies. They must develop aviation strategies in the same way as they develop economic strategies.

There are real constraints on the African aviation industry. In chapter four, we discussed the four levels at which different countries operate. Business champions will certainly find it easier to achieve success when they concentrate on countries where there is some level of existing infrastructure, the continental hubs and the emerging stars. This is where they'll find more opportunities to deploy their talents and uplift their industries. At the level of the traditional players and below, the average investor will experience so many challenges that they'll probably give up.

Yet, let's not overlook the fundamental importance of a genuine desire to effect change. Companies that have become champions are those that have started not with the ambition of creating a successful, government-backed enterprise, but those that have been driven since their inception by a desire to serve the African people and shift the business landscape on the continent. Ethiopian Airlines started with one old, tired aircraft; yet, today, the company operates an advanced fleet, including two $2 billion Dreamliners. NAS started in Kuwait and gradually expanded. Satguru was founded in Kigali and has grown to the point where it has offices in fifty countries.

The true differentiating factor, therefore, appears to be mindset. Champions challenge themselves to move beyond traditional ways of understanding and operating in Africa. They approach Africa with respect for the continent's unique strengths and possibilities, moving beyond common misconceptions. This mindset starts with company leaders and extends throughout organizations. Employees of Satguru generally describe the company's boss with respect and admiration, a combination rarely seen in other companies. The same is true at Ethiopian, where the leadership has made a big impact on the company's employees. Hassan might be too modest to claim the same of his tenure at NAS, but in Eric's eyes he, too, embodies the values of a charismatic leader. The drive to become a champion must be exemplified by the values of the company's leaders.

For African aviation to develop, the sector needs more people with determination and imagination. Susan Mashibe may be one of those people. She is taking a stand for aviation across the continent and doing so in a way that reverberates far beyond her own business. Mashibe is the founder and executive director of VIA Aviation, a flight support company that serves people wishing to charter private jets in Africa. Although VIA was founded in Tanzania, it has grown to include many other African countries. Due to VIA's success, Mashibe is recognized as one of the leaders in flight support services across the continent.

She was the first woman in Tanzania to hold both a Federal Aviation Administration-certified commercial pilot's license and an aircraft maintenance engineering qualification. Her clients include heads of state, *Fortune* 500 companies, celebrities, and military officials. Her first client was Jacob Zuma, the current president of South Africa, who contracted her services when he made an official visit to Tanzania. In 2011, the World Economic Forum recognized her achievements by naming her a Young Global Leader.

From an early age, Mashibe has been motivated by a genuine passion for aviation, which she traces back to an incident that occurred when she was four years old. Her parents and younger siblings departed for Dar es Salaam, leaving her alone with her grandmother. As she watched the plane carrying her family lift off, she didn't cry. Instead, she found herself wishing that she could fly the aircraft herself. That way, she reasoned, her parents would never leave her behind again. As she grew older, the experience stayed with her, inspiring her to study aviation.

Mashibe grew up in Arusha, a medium-sized city in Tanzania. Despite this humble background, she dreamed big and nurtured an ambitious vision for her life. When she founded her business, she used all her savings to rent a small office in Dar es Salaam Airport. Her company, which later became VIA, was named TanJet. Now, she runs her own company while also serving on the board of several international aviation organizations. Mashibe exemplifies the passion and vision that African aviation needs if it is to grow and stand comparison with other parts of the world.

For more champions to emerge, it's important that the right conditions exist. If you've ever watched professional team sports, you probably realize that the star players can't do everything alone. They need assistance from their teammates. In the same way, aviation in Africa needs both individual champions and sensible support from governments and regulatory bodies. Aviation can no longer be one small part of a broader conversation about infrastructure. It must be a priority of its own.

The true alchemy will happen when governments support the process of development, without artificially incentivizing it. Their job is not to subsidize companies that would otherwise fail, but to create the conditions in which people with vision can found and build companies. For this to happen, governments must decide what they really want from aviation. As of 2017, most governments in Africa haven't deeply considered this question. Until they do so, they aren't equipped to create the conditions necessary for private capital and human talent to flourish.

Let's look at an example of a country that is moving toward privatization and another that is heading in the opposite direction. The government of Madagascar founded Air Madagascar in 1947, shortly after the country achieved independence, and the airline commenced flights to France and South Africa in the 1960s and 1970s. Lufthansa Consulting was awarded a contract to help manage the company, which was acquiring aircraft and set on a growth agenda.

The airline's debts held it back, however, and after several efforts to restructure the deficit, the government decided to privatize the airline. That proved difficult: The political climate reduced passenger numbers, while the EU was concerned that the airline's aging fleet represented a danger and banned Air Madagascar from flying into Europe. In 2016, Air Madagascar employees staged a sit-in in opposition to privatization. Finally, in 2017, the airline announced that it had shortlisted two technical partners—Ethiopian Airlines and Air Austral, a French airline—as candidates to acquire a 49 percent stake in the airline. Ultimately, the government signed with Air Austral. At the time of writing, it's too soon to tell how well this move will work out.

By contrast, Tanzania, under President John Magufuli, is on

the other end of the spectrum. Speaking at a public gathering, President Magufuli told a cheering crowd that privatizing state-owned enterprises was wrong and had failed the country.[15] The airline was once privatized and partially owned by South African Airways. After it accumulated losses of US$20 million, however, the Tanzanian government bought back the shares.

Under a previous administration, Air Tanzania Company was earmarked for a second privatization. Under President Magufuli, the national carrier has been prioritized as a key infrastructure and tourism initiative, supporting the country's tourism sector that earns Tanzania about $2 billion in foreign currency annually. The airline is expected to receive four new aircraft in 2017—three from Canadian firm Bombardier and one 787 Dreamliner from Boeing. Again, it's too soon to tell how this move will pan out, although we have our doubts.

Many leaders are excited about the notion of jets with their country's name emblazoned on the side or about flying in business class. It's important to remember, however, that aviation is not a toy. It touches the lives of millions of people. To serve effectively, political leaders must understand the complexities of aviation. No amateur would try to perform their own surgery, yet governments too often seem to believe that, with little knowledge of the industry, they can found and operate an airline.

---

[15] Katare Mbashiru, "Tanzania: JPM—Privatization Was Wrong," *All Africa*, July 26, 2017, http://allafrica.com/stories/201707260222.html

In addition, private investors need the assurance that governments will honor contracts. In the past, this has been a common problem, with governments amending or canceling contracts as it suits them. Unless they can trust that governments take contracts seriously, companies will always be shy of committing to investment. With a combination of improving conditions and visionary private sector leaders, the potential of Africa can truly be realized. It's time for the continent to rise.

CHAPTER NINE

THE AGENDA FOR AVIATION IN AFRICA

This chapter focuses on the role governments must play to encourage champions and shape a dynamic African aviation sector. It may seem simple to say that African aviation must be liberalized; indeed, this was agreed when the Yamoussoukro Decision was taken back in the 1990s. The intervening years, however, have brought little progress. Liberalization will lead to three valuable outcomes: new routes and more frequent flights, better connections, and lower fares. These three improvements will encourage an increase in the number of passengers, which will have positive effects, both directly and indirectly, on trade, business travel, and tourism. This, in turn, will impact the broader economy, generating more tourism revenue, job growth, and productivity and ultimately enhancing both the GDP of African countries and the welfare of ordinary Africans.

As of 2017, there is still a long way to go before most countries in Africa are effectively liberalized. Many leaders maintain protectionist policies. These countries tend to impede liberalization, creating discriminatory practices to shield small or uncompetitive national carriers from the vagaries of the market, a practice that remains prevalent all over the continent.

In some cases, unfair restrictions have been placed on African airlines by non-African companies. While safety and security concerns are often cited as the reasons for these restrictions, they may also be economically motivated. Airlines such as Air France, KLM, and SN Brussels generate a lot of revenue on their African routes because the tickets prices are some of the highest in the world, making them adverse to encouraging local competition.

Another barrier to aviation progress in Africa is the continuing difficulty of obtaining visas. African countries operate some of the most restrictive visa policies in the world. If the sector is to be fully liberalized, a concerted continent-wide effort to loosen visa restrictions must play a role.

In 2014, InterVISTAS Consulting authored a report titled, *Trans-*

forming Intra-African Air Connectivity: The Economic Benefits of Implementing the Yamoussoukro Decision. The report explains that "The total number of seats operated between the EU and Morocco increased by 160 percent between 2005 and 2013 and the number of routes operated between points in the EU and points in Morocco rose from 83 in 2005 to 309 in 2013. While part of this is due to the entry of low-cost carriers like EasyJet, Fastjet, and Air Arabia, it is also due to the Morocco-EU Open Skies Agreement, which was signed in 2006." The same study analyzed twelve different African countries to determine the potential economic impact of liberalization. In South Africa alone, the study's authors estimated that liberalization could yield fifteen thousand new jobs and generate US$284 million in GDP.

In addition to liberalization, it's essential for African nations to separate the roles of regulator and operator in the aviation sector, in line with global best practice. Regulators enforce civil aviation policy, while operators handle the running of airports. They each have an important role to play, but those roles shouldn't become confused or intertwined. In countries that operate a national carrier, this should also be operated separately. In too many African countries, two or three of these functions are merged, hampering economic development and negatively impacting quality.

In some instances, national laws discourage investment. In

Malawi, for example, it's illegal for a foreign airline or private investor to own more than 49 percent of a national airline. This prevented Ethiopian from purchasing more than a 49 percent stake in Malawian Airlines. Laws of this type hinder foreign investment because they prevent investors from assuming control of their investments. For many, this is naturally a priority, especially when the amounts of money involved are substantial.

Challenges such as these are spread across the continent. Few countries have both ratified and implemented the Yamoussoukro Decision. Ethiopia, as you might expect, has come closest. The country offers all other African nations reciprocal agreements, essentially giving the carriers of other nations whatever privileges those countries extend to Ethiopian. This is one reason why Ethiopian is well received almost everywhere on the continent. Not a single country, however, has fully liberalized their skies in compliance with the Yamoussoukro Decision. If this were to become commonplace across the continent, it would result in reduced fares, better connectivity, improved passenger convenience, more punctuality, and greater reliability.

As a follow-up to the Yamoussoukro Decision, twenty-three African nations have signed a Declaration of Solemn Commitment toward the establishment of a single African air transport market by 2017. Whereas the Yamoussoukro Decision was initially signed by forty-four countries, the Declaration of Solemn Commitment was initially signed by eleven, with twelve more following after the AU Summit of 2015 in Addis Ababa. The African Civil Aviation Commission is tasked with the responsibility of crafting the finer details of the agreement.

While it's a little too soon to assess the progress of the declaration in depth, many of the signatories are countries we have mentioned in these pages as existing leaders or emerging stars, who have already demonstrated commitment to aviation. These include South Africa, Ethiopia, Egypt, Kenya, Rwanda, and Côte d'Ivoire. This leads us to believe that it has a good chance of success.

Aviation is important, especially to us, but other transport infrastructure will also play a large role in driving growth in Africa. Also at the AU Summit in 2015, China signed a memorandum with the union committing to connecting all major African cities by rail and highway, Africa's most substantive agreement with any partner.

Tearing down barriers to the development of aviation is essential to the growth of the sector. Boeing and Airbus are leaders in aircraft manufacturing because they have long been supported by cooperative governments. For Africa to become a significant player in the aviation sector, the continent's leaders must create the conditions in which companies can grow and develop without needless bureaucracy.

In 2004, Eric visited India. India has a reputation for bureaucracy and cumbersome government regulations, a legacy of the British Raj. Yet, Eric visited ten cities over the course of two weeks, at a total cost of US$500. He flew with one of India's low-cost carriers and employed a helpful Indian travel agent to book his flights, hotels, and activities. Wherever he landed, local drivers were available for hire. As he explored India's cities, he was struck by how many of the travelers around him were domestic: Indians traveling within India.

Admittedly, India is a single country, whereas Africa is an entire continent. Nonetheless, India's population is approximately 1.1 billion people, which is comparable to all of Africa. Additionally, India is a very diverse place, with numerous distinct regions and languages. It became a unified country only in 1947, with the rather arbitrary division created by Partition. In many ways, therefore, India and Africa are similar. India is much smaller than Africa, but both are developing regions addressing many of the same problems. While Africa has continued to suffer from protectionism, however, there has been a general recognition in India that improving aviation will lift the whole country to do better. This mindset has been used to drive a unified aviation policy. We believe that Africa deserves a similar approach.

AVIATION FOR EVERYONE

As this book has described, there are already some positive developments in African aviation. Some countries, such as

Côte d'Ivoire and Rwanda, are making strategic bets in the sector, employing best practices to drive vibrant aviation growth. Similarly, some entrepreneurs, such as Susan Mashibe, are already making a mark. Companies such as NAS are pioneering models—for instance, public-private partnerships—that are still rare in Africa and have the potential to revolutionize the financing of infrastructure. Due to these changes, investors are taking the potential of aviation in Africa seriously. Each of these elements signposts the way toward a bright future.

If African aviation is to build on these foundations, it will need to address the challenges of scale. It makes more sense to invest in support services across several airports than it does to invest in one. The margins for catering companies become more attractive when they serve more than fifty meals per day. Why does NAS send managers to be trained in Kuwait, instead of training them in Africa? Because the scale of aviation in Africa is not yet large enough for world-class training schools to be readily accessible across much of the continent.

We envisage an aviation sector in which African citizens see flying as an easy, cheap, and convenient form of travel, much as the citizens of North America do. In the United States, aviation supports both business and leisure travel. Flights are affordable, most cities are connected to one another, and people find it easy to book their travel online. In many cases, it's easier and more economical to fly than to drive. There's no reason why

Africa can't seek to emulate at least some aspects of the aviation sector in more developed economies.

For this to happen, however, global best practices must be applied across the continent. Too many African countries continue to view aviation as a single industry, thereby placing a single body in charge of the airport, civil aviation, the national carrier, and anything else related to the sector. That's a policy that lacks checks and balances and reflects a fundamental misunderstanding of the sector. For aviation in Africa to become a universal method of travel, all these functions must be separated.

There is also huge potential for African companies to develop stronger partnerships with European counterparts. In many cases, European companies already own a minority stake in African aviation companies. Air France-KLM, for example, holds a 26 percent share in Kenya Airways and 20 percent in Air Côte d'Ivoire. While the imagined benefits of this type of international partnership haven't always transpired, there is potential to do far more.

European partners provide a pipeline of experienced professionals, who can either manage part of an African operation or train local people. They also provide access to capital and established reputations, which African companies can trade on. European companies already have relationships with suppliers, so they can leverage economies of scale. This applies when they are negotiating with other airlines, customers, aircraft manufacturers, and equipment suppliers.

A key to making aviation more accessible in Africa will be the reduction of taxes. At present, they are among the highest in the world. This translates into unnecessarily high ticket prices, because suppliers, from travel agents and airlines to support service companies and airport security services, pass taxes and fees along to passengers. Worse, the application of these taxes often appears arbitrary and paying them is inconvenient.

In 2011, Hassan flew from Zanzibar to Dar es Salaam. After checking in, he received a boarding pass and proceeded to security. At security, he was told that he needed to go to the bank. Why? Because he was required to pay a $100 departure tax. He wasn't carrying $100 and he hadn't been informed about the tax in advance, but the response to his frustrations was unsympathetic. He was told bluntly that he had to pay $100 in cash, denominated in US dollars. Credit cards and local currency weren't accepted.

Aside from the expense and inconvenience, policies such as this one erode goodwill. In Europe, Hassan could have spent that same $100 on flying from Paris to London with a low-cost carrier such as Ryanair or easyJet.

If aviation is a privilege for the select few, imposing a $100 tax makes sense. It's a way to claim additional revenue from people who can undoubtedly afford it. If, however, aviation is to grow and bring Africans the benefits we've discussed in this book, this mindset must change. It deters the middle classes from flying, preventing the benefits of aviation from permeating society.

Governments needn't even lose income from reducing taxes. Instead of taxing a small number of wealthy people $100, they could be taxing ten times as many people $10, while simultaneously boosting both the aviation sector and all the other industries that benefit, directly and indirectly, from aviation. More people flying means more economic activity and ultimately more revenue for governments. Changes such as this, however, require vision and initiative from regulators.

This effect can be seen in other sectors. The SMART Africa initiative, headquartered in Rwanda, successfully pushed through reforms that led to the abolition of roaming fees across East Africa. At first, mobile operators protested the potential lost revenue. Within a year, however, they found that call volume had multiplied by five times.

When customers were forced to pay roaming fees, they simply limited themselves to local calls and local service providers. Only a small percentage of customers ever paid the roaming fees. Thanks to the reforms, far more people are calling regionally, boosting the revenue of operators even as people feel freer to connect with far-flung relatives and friends. Traffic between Rwanda and Uganda has grown by 800 percent. Between Rwanda and Kenya, it has grown by 400 percent. Between Rwanda and South Sudan, where mobile traffic used to be practically nonexistent, it has grown by over 1,000 percent.

This example illustrates what could happen in aviation. If air travel becomes more affordable, more people will fly. As a result, cooperation across Africa will grow, as increasing numbers of travelers create more demand for goods and services. That demand will enable players in the industry to operate at further accelerating the development of aviation while satisfying government requirements for tax revenue.

As the demand for aviation services increases, so will the demand for skilled workers. Flying an aircraft requires a high level of skill, as does converting an airport into a shopping mall or ensuring that services are conveniently packaged. African nations have typically struggled in service industries, because workers have lacked the requisite skills due to a lack of education or training. As the sector grows, people who can regulate and work in the industry will become essential.

Serving this increasing demand will have the effect of boosting the overall skill levels of African workers. People who have performed a skilled role in one sector are more apt to adapt if they wish to change careers or to relocate. In 2017, African airline workers are often limited in their options. An employee of Air Côte d'Ivoire who wishes to leave the company but remain in the airline industry will find themselves very short of options. There are no other airlines in Côte d'Ivoire. If they wish to find a new role, they will be forced to leave the country.

The same is true for a person working in ground handling. There is only one ground handling company, NAS, operating in Côte d'Ivoire. Anyone wishing to leave NAS but remain in the industry will find that they have few alternatives, even if they have ten to twenty years of experience. An engineer working for Ethiopian Airlines is in a similar position. In truth, this situation is common to many markets. Many industries have high barriers to entry and limited options, hampering the movement of specialized labor.

We'd like to see this change, however, to aid the transmission of valuable skills and experience. Earlier we described a friend of ours, who started in a junior position with Satguru and worked his way up to head an entire region. He is incredibly skilled at finding flight routes and figuring out how to get people where they want to go. Almost anyone can learn to use a booking system, but proficiency in providing solutions-driven travel agency is about more than learning how to use a system. It's about taking a skill and turning it into a craft. Our friend knows how to place himself in the shoes of a traveler, anticipating both possibilities and pitfalls. Much of what he does can't be learned from formal training. It takes a combination of talent, passion, and experience.

Now imagine that he was trapped in a job that didn't give him the opportunity to exercise or share his skills. He would be incredibly frustrated, and others would miss out on everything he could have shared with them. Liberalizing aviation in Africa promises to create more opportunities for talented people, increasing the chances that they can find a niche in which they can shine.

WHAT ARE THE NEXT STEPS?

As we conclude this chapter, we'll leave you with our top recommendations of policy improvements that need to be instigated if African aviation is to fulfill its enormous potential. First, the Yamoussoukro Decision must be implemented and open skies policies must become the norm across the continent. As discussed at length, poor connectivity often makes flying in Africa a frustrating and exhausting experience. More direct flights would alleviate the frustration and make travel far more pleasant. The Yamoussoukro Decision shows that governments understand what it will take for aviation in Africa to flourish. The next challenge is to go beyond talk into implementation.

Second, there must be greater separation of regulatory bodies from operating companies. This is essential for the independence of regulatory bodies and to allow operators to focus on running their businesses as profitable concerns. Similarly, it's essential that national carriers are independent of government and allowed to flourish as private enterprises. Owning and operating an airline is a commercial decision and should be treated as such.

For the same reason, governments should actively invite the participation of the private sector in all commercial areas of the aviation sector. This goes hand in hand with our fifth recommendation: the creation of a legal framework that protects investors. When investors enter into partnerships lasting ten, fifteen, or twenty years, they want to know that their rights will be respected in the event of a change of government or another unexpected change in circumstances. In 2017, many African countries don't guarantee this level of transparency and accountability.

The sixth policy shift we'd like to see is greater access to essential insurance products and safety innovations. It's important that safety regulations are stringently and uniformly applied. Aviation accidents are both tragic and costly. It's vital to take steps both to prevent them and to minimize their impact in worst-case scenarios. From the perspective of passengers, booking a flight with an African airline may feel like a considerable risk. A handful of African carriers have strong track records for delivering safety and reliability. Most do not.

Finally, we'd like to see dramatic changes in visa and immigration policies. If people cannot enter the countries they wish to visit, growth in the aviation sector becomes almost impossible. At present, obtaining work permits and employing talented people can be a huge challenge, which deters investment and growth. Anything that encourages the free movement of goods and people across the continent will make a considerable difference. A more cooperative approach will also allow security services to coordinate and exchange information more easily. The types of security threats that exist globally are also prevalent in Africa, so it's critical that reforms are enacted as soon as possible.

Ultimately, these proposals are only a request that governments exercise leadership in their roles as regulators. Africa needs leaders who are willing to prioritize aviation and deliver policy changes that nourish the sector. There's a lot of hard work ahead to create a level playing field, convincing private investors that African aviation is a good destination for their money and encouraging champions-in-waiting to believe that their dreams can become reality.

CONCLUSION

A NEW VISION

What can growth in aviation do for the average citizen of Africa? Aviation has already allowed people like us, your authors, to leave our hometowns and study elsewhere in the world. It has allowed us to travel across the continent and beyond, learning and growing. It supports our careers and our lives. Aviation can play a huge role in making the AUC's Agenda 2063 a reality, changing lives across the continent and supporting trade growth, both within Africa and intercontinentally.

Looking ahead, we see opportunities both to reinforce existing hubs and to build aviation ecosystems in places without major hubs. Will we see the emergence of new hubs and low-cost carriers? In West Africa, the jury is still out, although Abidjan and Dakar are contenders. Morocco is well positioned to thrive in the coming years, while Rwanda is positioning itself to become a bridge between East and Central Africa and the rest of the world. It's hard to predict which cities will stake claims as hubs in years to come, but we're confident that the first countries to reliably support low-cost carriers will position themselves for success.

Aviation can play a tremendous role in helping Africa to turn potential into real prosperity. Yet, it's a sector that requires many different, connected industries to work together. All the different elements, including infrastructure, support, and packaging services, must develop in a coordinated fashion. For this to happen, private capital has a vital role to play. It's the champions and the investors who will inspire others by demonstrating what's possible. Governments, meanwhile, must demonstrate a greater appetite for liberalization making and enforcing rules that are conducive to the growth of the sector.

With a combination of infrastructure, legislation, and quality support services, the pieces will be in place for African aviation to soar. We believe that the future of aviation lies in Africa. As the continent grows and economies continue to develop, we will see more and more opportunities for new business models to be born on the continent. Africa has much to learn, but it also has much to teach. With vision, cooperation, and commitment, we believe Africa's aviation potential will be fully realized.

ACKNOWLEDGMENTS

HASSAN

I wish to extend my appreciation to the men and women who have come from all over the world to work for National Aviation Services (NAS), serve the airports in which we operate, handle the flights of our esteemed airline customers, and provide their passengers and cargo with a high level of service and efficiency. These people work around the clock every day of the year, including holidays, through scorching summer heat and extreme winter snow, all to ensure that the world's aviation ecosystems remain vibrant and alive. For their commitment and loyalty, they have my heartfelt gratitude.

ERIC

A few African countries inspired us to write this book thanks to their investment in aviation. Ethiopia is one of such country, as are Rwanda, Kenya, and my own country, Côte d'Ivoire. They show that it is possible for Africa to excel in the difficult sector that is aviation.

I would like to express my gratitude to the editors and support team involved in this project. Without their support, this book would not have become a reality.

Writing a book means taking precious hours away from family. My eternal gratitude goes to my wife, Darline, for her patience and support while I took time away from her and our daughter, Maria. Without her, this book may never have reached fruition.

ABOUT THE AUTHORS

ERIC KACOU holds an MPA from the Harvard Kennedy School and an MBA from the Wharton School of the University of Pennsylvania. Eric is cofounder and CEO of Entrepreneurial Solutions Partners (ESP), an advisory and investment firm serving entrepreneurs and leaders across Africa. In 2010, he was recognized as a Young Global Leader by the World Economic Forum in Davos as well as an Archbishop Desmond Tutu Fellow by the African Leadership Institute (ALI). His first book, Entrepreneurial Solutions for Prosperity in BoP Markets, was published in January 2011.

HASSAN EL-HOURY holds an MBA from the Wharton School of the University of Pennsylvania and a BBA from the American University of Beirut. He is the group CEO of National Aviation Services (NAS), the fastest-growing aviation services provider in the Middle East, India, and Africa. He is also a board director with various large companies in emerging markets. In 2014, he was named a Young Global Leader by the World Economic Forum in Davos, in recognition of his contributions to aviation and airport services.